G000061019

RAFTER: Figs. 1-5. Inclined member of a pitched roof, running from top of external wall (eaves) to roof apex (ridge), to support roof covering. RIDGE: Figs. 1-6. The apex of a pitched roof. WALL PLATE: Fig. 1. Timber member laid on wall to take feet of rafters (or ends of joists), and distribute weight along wall. SPROCKET: Fig. 2. A short rafter sometimes attached to feet of common rafters, but laid at lower pitch, to give upward sweep to roof. PARAPET: Fig. 3. A wall formed by the extension of an external wall above its point of junction either with a pitched or flat roof. COUPLE ROOF: Fig. 1. The simplest pitched roof construction, rafters supporting the roof unaided. COLLAR ROOF: Fig. 4. A stronger roof with wooden ties fastening opposing rafters. TRUSSED ROOF: Fig. 5. Buildings wider than 18 feet usually need a longitudinal beam to support the common rafters, and such a beam is called a ‘purlin’. Purlins may rest on cross walls, or be carried by triangular girders, called Roof Trusses. EAVES: The lowest part of a roof, overhanging the wall. EAVES CORNICE: Fig. 6. A projecting moulding at eaves level. DORMER: Fig. 6. A window projecting from a pitched roof. VERGE: Fig. 6. The slight projection of a pitched roof covering beyond the end (or gable) wall. GABLE: Fig. 6. Triangular-shaped end wall formed by the two sloping roof sides at the end of a ridged roof. STRING COURSE: Fig. 6. A horizontal band, plain or moulded, on the face of a structure. PLINTH: Fig. 6. The projecting base of a structure. CANOPY or HOOD: Fig. 6. A projection or roof, frequently over a doorway. CASEMENT WINDOW: Fig. 7. One with glazed portions secured in a metal or wood framework which may be fixed, or hinged or pivoted to open. SASH WINDOW: Fig. 7. One with the glazed portions divided horizontally, each secured in a wooden framework, sliding in vertical side grooves, assisted by counter-weights. MULLION: Fig. 7. An upright member dividing a window. TRANSOME: Fig. 7. A horizontal member dividing a window. HEAD: Fig. 7. The topmost horizontal member of a window or door frame. CILL: Fig. 7. The lowest horizontal member of a window or door frame. HIPPED ROOF: Fig. 8. A pitched roof of which the end is formed by a sloping roof. HIP: Fig. 8. The line of intersection of two sloping roofs when the angle roofed within the buildings is less than 180 degrees. VALLEY: Fig. 8. The line of intersection of two sloping roofs, when the angle roofed within the building is greater than 180 degrees. OUTSHUT: Fig. 8. A small extension to a building, roofed by carrying down the main slope in a CATSLIDE. QUOIN: Fig. 8. The external angle of a building.

COUPLE ROOF

1

SPROCKETS

2

PARAPETS

3

COLLAR ROOF

4

TRUSSED ROOF

5

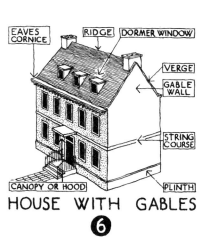

HOUSE WITH GABLES

6

CASEMENT   SASH

WINDOWS

7

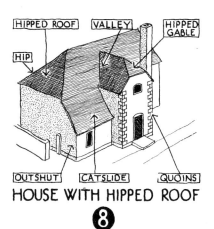

HOUSE WITH HIPPED ROOF

8

ABBREVIATIONS OF NAMES USED ON PLANS IN THIS BOOK.				
E.C. = EARTH CLOSET.	CO. = COOKER.	C. = CUPBOARD.	Br. = BROOMS.	B. = BATH.
W.C. = WATER CLOSET.	L.A. = LARDER.	L. = LAVATORY BASIN.	D. = DRESSER.	S. = SINK.

HOUSES

MARGARET & ALEXANDER POTTER

JOHN MURRAY

ACKNOWLEDGEMENTS

We wish to thank the following architects for allowing us to make illustrations of their work: Messrs A. V. Pilley and B. Lubetkin (four houses on page 38); W. A. Eden (Council houses on pages 38 and 39); D. Lasdun (house on pages 40 and 41); F. Gibberd (houses on pages 42 and 43); Tecton (flats on pages 44 and 45); and the architect to the London County Council (the Brandon Estate page 46). We acknowledge gratefully generous assistance from the late Professor Budden; and Messrs R. H. Williams, A. V. Pilley, the late C. G. Dobson, W. Braxton Sinclair, J. Mansell Jenkinson, and W. A. Eden, and the Bournville Village Trust Architects Department. We also wish to thank the National Building Agency for permission to illustrate Uplands Estate, Holly Street, Warley on the front of the jacket (bottom illustration) and to reproduce diagrams 2 and 3 on page 48; and the British Standards Institution for permission to redraw diagram 4 on page 48 and the perspective of a dimensionally co-ordinated room on the back of the jacket (bottom illustration) from *Basic Space for Structure External Envelope and Internal Sub-division*. Finally, we should like to thank the many kind people who without any introduction allowed us to examine and measure their houses.

By the same authors
INTERIORS

First edition 1948
Second edition 1960
Third edition 1973

© Margaret and Alexander Potter 1960, 1973

Printed in Great Britain by W. S. Cowell Ltd, London and Ipswich.

0 7195 2812 7

AUTHORS' PREFACE

YOU may object, to begin with, that we have used the word 'Houses' in the title and have proceeded to draw huts, shacks, tenements, flats, houses, a castle and a manor. They are all 'dwellings' but the word is pretentious; 'places to live in', while it strikes the right note, takes rather many words to do so.

Apart from the castle and the manor, whose presence we will explain later, all these places to live in were occupied by people of average or below average means. This has meant that we have had to ignore the fine design and craftsmanship that went into many of the great houses.

It is all a question of what we set out to do. Most of us see so many houses every day that an attempt to explain their differences would alone be sufficient purpose for this book. But we felt that a better object was to examine the changing shape of houses as a guide to planning our future homes. As the greatest numbers of new houses are likely to be of medium size or smaller, it follows that our study would be most usefully confined to houses of this type.

To set the scene we have three pages of feudal housing—a castle, a manor and a hut. Then, since there is insufficient information to treat all earlier houses in detail, we begin the book proper with a Fifteenth Century house and from there the procession continues down to the present-day house.

The usual arrangement has been to examine typical buildings of each century, devoting a double-page to each house. We have tried to show as clearly as possible the construction of the houses, and we have not been afraid to introduce technical terms where they were helpful. An explanation of unfamiliar terms will be found on the front endpaper, and the back endpaper sets out and illustrates some details of building processes. On page 7, we have summarized the various ways of constructing a house and on pages 8 and 9 give a map to show where traditional building materials are to be found in this country.

Other books have been published which set out the development of the house, and some of them contain excellent photographs. There are three reasons why we chose drawings in preference to photographs. Firstly, because most old buildings have been very much altered and only a drawing could attempt to reconstruct them as they were originally built; secondly, we wanted sometimes to remove the outer skins of buildings, to reveal the construction; and finally, in order to show the buildings in use, we have included in the drawings some of the inhabitants of the various houses.

The text set in the same type as this Preface reads from page to page straight through the book. Notes in small italics give more technical details and are independent of the main story.

AUTHORS' PREFACE TO THE THIRD EDITION

THE preparation of this new edition of *Houses* has brought a flood of memories, notably of miles and miles of cycling in tandem along the roads of the mid-1940's, searching out the houses from which to make our choice. The roads were nearly always deserted, silent except for country sounds; the houses, when we found them, had changed little from the time of their completion. Sanitation was rudimentary save in the more recently built houses; domestic and personal washing facilities were meagre. Central heating was scarcely a dream. Not only the countryside, its fields and hedges and its ancient houses, seemed immutable; so did the crafts of building. One day, after sketching a house built in 1618, we came across men nearby who were sorting and trimming stone slates. The roof for which these slates were intended differed little from that built in 1618. As we drew the men at their work they talked about their craft.

Houses was very nearly as much a craft production as many of the buildings it illustrates. The line drawings were made with scratchy steel nibs, chalks were applied to the drawings to provide shades and shadows; each colour area was greased on to individual lithographic plates and all the labels were hand-drawn. In consequence, our book may itself have acquired something of a period flavour.

Now, in 1973, there are few traditional craftsmen left. Most natural materials, such as clay tiles, slates, thatch and stone, are no longer in use for new construction. Building processes have changed and are changing fast. The hand-made and the one-off have been superseded by the machined and the mass-produced. This innovation distinguishes the present from all earlier ages. Changes in building have been numerous: in materials from timber to brick, in style from Gothic to Renaissance; but the thread of craftsmanship and the use of materials which mellowed with age was constant. Now the thread has snapped. To-day's materials and techniques are no better and no worse than those used by our ancestors. Intrinsically, however, many of them differ radically from those of earlier building ages.

Some of the main features of this revolutionary change are indicated on page 48, which has been written for the new edition. It seemed desirable to use modern drawing techniques for the new illustrations. So we cleaned out our patent non-clogging reservoir nibbed pens, filled them with special non-clog ink, took our stick-down shading sheets and our paste-on lettering and set to work. Whether the new methods are quicker than the old is a moot point. About the increased costs we have no doubt.

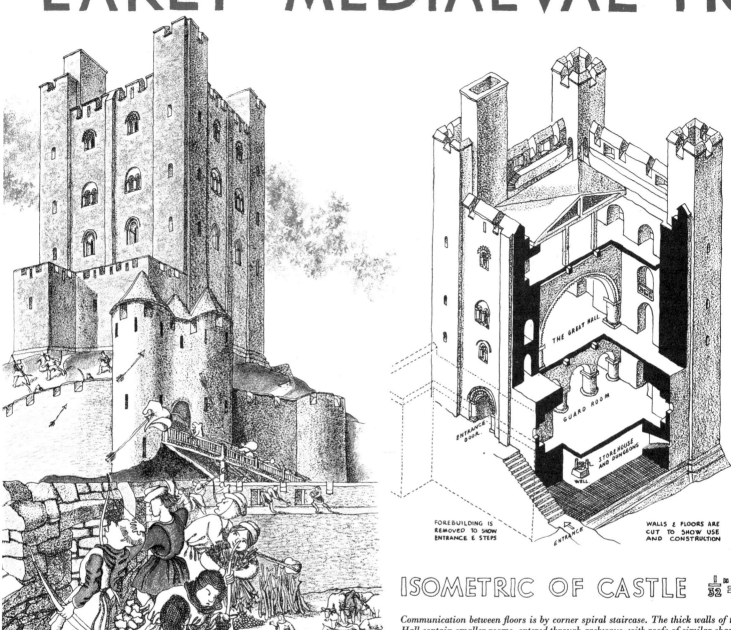

PERSPECTIVE OF CASTLE

ISOMETRIC OF CASTLE $\frac{1}{32}$

Communication between floors is by corner spiral staircase. The thick walls of th
Hall contain smaller rooms, entered through archways, with roofs of similar shape
like stone tunnels—known as barrel vaults. This construction was impossible for th
main roof, as the space of about 30-ft. by 40-ft. was too big. A large beam, centr
across the narrower way might have been used, but 30-ft. was a long length
handle. Instead an arch was used for spanning the Hall, carrying the ends of 20-f
long beams, reaching from the external walls. The arch also helps support the roo
Below, where space is less valuable, three simpler arches are used, and on th
ground floor there would be a wall with doors. The well was inside for times of sieg

THE SAXONS built in timber, and this largely accounts for the fact that little is left to tell us about their houses. The Normans brough
with them from France the idea of the fortified private house, and though the earliest were made of timber, surrounded by wooden pallisade
it was not long before they began to construct the stone castles for which they are famous. The earlier castles often had two rooms side b
side on the first floor, an arrangement which we call a Hall-Keep. The larger room was known as the Hall and was used by everybody; th
smaller was called the Chamber and was the owner's private room. Steps, built inside for safety, led down from the first floor to the groun
floor which was used as a storehouse and might contain dungeons. Another, and probably later arrangement, has the Chamber above th
Hall, and this arrangement is known as a Tower-Keep. Our example is of this type, but has an additional floor.

The Norman castle was clearly a fortress as well as a home, and most of them were built during the Twelfth Century when the oppositio
to the Normans in this country was at its most intense. Easily defensible sites such as headlands or hillocks would be selected whereve
possible, but artificial mounds were sometimes made and these would be surrounded by dry ditches spanned by wooden approach bridge

The early castle shown in the small drawing is of the Twelfth-century type, has stone walls in place of the early wooden pallisade
and an outer court or bailey. Towards the end of the Thirteenth Century new castles were built as fortifications against the Welsh. Ou
small drawing of a later castle shows one of this period, and has outer walls, called List Walls, built to keep more powerful offensive weapo
at a greater distance. It is surrounded by a water moat, which would be good protection against gunpowder mining. The Gate House is th
largest part of the castle, and takes the place of the Keep. It often houses the portcullis and machinery for working the drawbridge. Th
smaller building defending the approach to the bridge is called a Barbican.

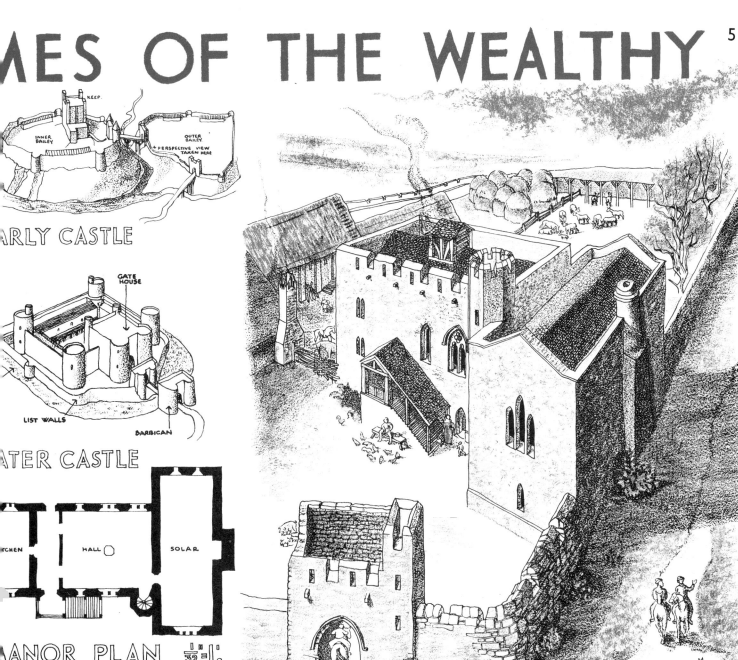

ARLY CASTLE

KEEP

INNER BAILEY

OUTER BAILEY

PERSPECTIVE VIEW TAKEN HERE

ATER CASTLE

GATE HOUSE

LIST WALLS

BARBICAN

ANOR PLAN $\frac{1}{32} = 1'$

TCHEN   HALL   SOLAR

ike the Castle Walls, those of the Manor are of stone, arrying the roof, and most of the floor weight. First oors were sometimes supported on wooden cross beams, t other times by arches or vaults with a central row of round floor columns. For supporting the roof of the ong shaped Manor hall, the usual arrangement was to mploy cross beams and trusses, to pick up the roof eight and transfer it to the walls. Roof coverings were tone slabs, or wooden chips called 'shingles', or thatch.

PERSPECTIVE VIEW OF MANOR HOUSE

As time went on there was less fighting and, by the end of Edward I's reign, great houses were being built with reduced fortifications. Our drawing represents a Thirteenth Century stone manor house. The large room, or Hall, was still used by everybody, and it usually had a fire in the centre with a ventilator in the roof for the smoke to escape. A private room, called a Solar, was provided at one end of the Hall for the Lord of the Manor, and a kitchen was often built at the other end. These principal rooms were still to be found on the first floor, approached by an outer staircase, and the ground floor made convenient storage space for winter food stocks. You will see how little the arrangement differs from that of the castle.

The Hall and Solar would be lofty rooms and a very common plan was to use this height to build a servants' dormitory above the kitchen, an open ladder leading to it from the Hall. Many farmers built themselves houses of this pattern, on a somewhat smaller scale, during the late Fourteenth and Fifteenth Centuries, which was a time of increasing prosperity for them.

As the drawing shows, the manor has windows of the kind we expect to see in churches. Since in mediæval times stone was the building material for both churches and manors, the same method was used for spanning the window openings. The small stones were built into rch forms, first rounded as we show in the castle, and later pointed. The earliest pointed windows were simply slits like most of those in he drawing of the manor, but more complicated ones were built at a later period. We have imagined the Lord of this Manor following he fashion and building in new windows to shed more light at the end of his Hall, where he sat on a dais to eat his meals.

The sanitary arrangements, if any, were simple; the mediæval equivalent of a water-closet was to make a downward shaft in the thickness f the wall, discharging into a pit below or into the moat.

A POORER HOUSE

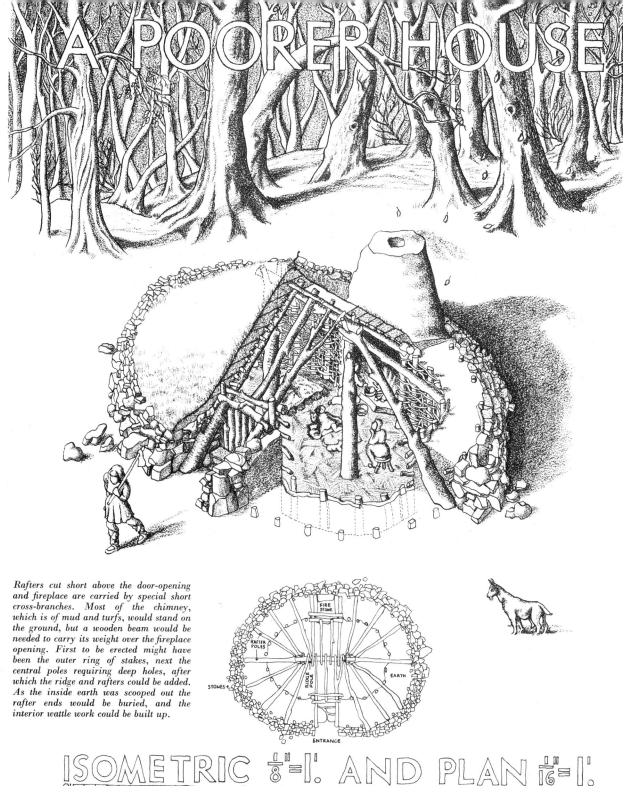

Rafters cut short above the door-opening and fireplace are carried by special short cross-branches. Most of the chimney, which is of mud and turfs, would stand on the ground, but a wooden beam would be needed to carry its weight over the fireplace opening. First to be erected might have been the outer ring of stakes, next the central poles requiring deep holes, after which the ridge and rafters could be added. As the inside earth was scooped out the rafter ends would be buried, and the interior wattle work could be built up.

FIRE STONE
RAFTER POLES
STONES
RIDGE POLE
EARTH
ENTRANCE

ISOMETRIC ⅛"=1'. AND PLAN 1/16"=1'.

FOLLOWING the Norman Conquest, farmers continued to cultivate the land on the old Open Field system under their new masters. Compared with the castles which they helped to build, their own homes were built of flimsy materials. The house shown here is conjectural. Despite the large number of excavations carried out we have little exact knowledge of the humbler dwellings built before 1200 A.D. The building techniques of the time would not have been new. Huts like the one shown above would have been common at much earlier periods and doubtless survived as work places to a much later date.

The earliest hut-type house was probably circular with a vertical central pole; inclined branches (called rafters) stuck in the ground rested against the centre-pole at the top. This formed a rough framework for the outer roof-covering of thatch. Our picture shows a later form of this type of hut. It has two upright poles with a horizontal branch between them (a ridge), against which the rafters lean from the sides of the hut. The ground inside the hut would be scooped out to give extra headroom and to provide soil to be used as ballast to prevent the rafter ends from slipping outwards. The earth was often cut away on the outside, providing better drainage. On the inner side of the earth wall we show a framework of wattles, which makes it possible to pack the earth tightly. Wattles were also used between the rafters to carry the roof-covering. A fairly good roof could be obtained by cutting turfs slantways, and laying them upside down as in the drawing. The vegetable matter provided a strong bed, and the inclined cutting made a snug fit. Turf chimneys were used in Welsh border counties in the Nineteenth Century but may well have existed very much earlier. Such a chimney would be the first part of a house to be erected, since once in use it established the builder's right to his site.

BUILDING SYSTEMS

HAVING briefly sketched in the position prior to the Fifteenth Century, we give a more detailed account of the smaller house of the centuries following. Examples of town and country building, detached and attached housing, are set out in the sequence in which they came widely into use, or in which they are for other reasons important to our survey.

Up to the Eighteenth and Nineteenth Centuries, local builders used the material nearest to hand. On pages 8 and 9 we have made a map showing the distribution of natural building materials, but as in our survey we can treat only the commonest of these, we have surrounded the map with drawings of houses built with a variety of local materials, some of which we have not had space to examine in detail later.

Here common building systems are explained diagrammatically and illustrated by reference to the houses we examine in the rest of the book. Earliest come the timber buildings; the 'cruck' with no structural walls at all and roof nearly to the ground; and the timber frame, in which the strength is in the frame, the panels serving only to keep out the weather. This construction was in some districts used as late as the Eighteenth Century, although no longer fashionable.

Throughout the Middle Ages men looked back to Roman times as to a superior age. One of the evidences of classical superiority was that they built houses, as well as public buildings, of stone. Therefore, when the growth of trade once more made the building of stone houses possible, generally it appeared as an improvement. Hence plaster and wood gave way to brick and stone, and houses of this type are still very popular to-day. Reinforced concrete had a following before the war because it allowed big windows and great freedom in spacing inside walls. To-day it is even more widely used for spanning wide openings, for frame buildings, and for constructing floors and roofs.

Most plans are drawn to the same scale (1/16th of an inch to one foot) for the purposes of comparison.

FRAME

Fig. 1 shows a structural analysis of the timber framed house of pages 14 and 15. Fig. 2 is the reinforced concrete house of pages 40 and 41. Their structural systems are the same, but different materials have been used. The remaining timber framed examples are on pages 8—house letter B; 9—house letters F and G; and page 10. Other reinforced concrete houses or flats are on pages 38 and 44. If the structural systems on this page are compared and understood, together with the examples of each type, it will give some idea of the bearing that structural systems and materials have upon appearance.

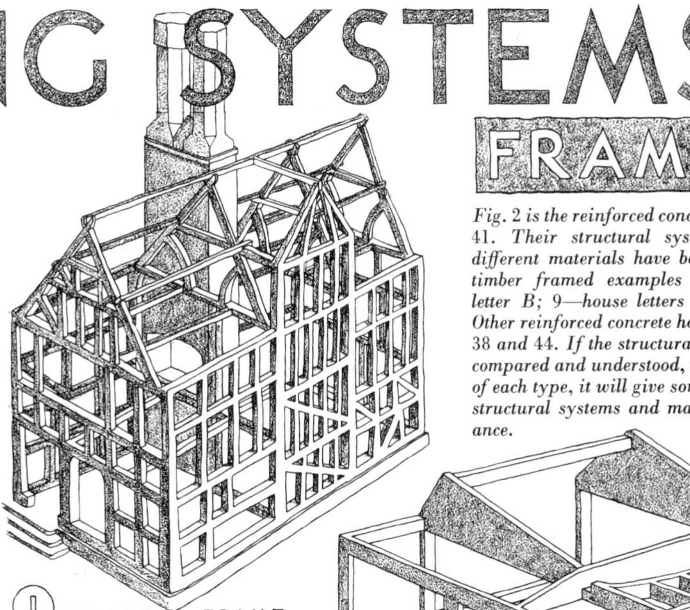

① TIMBER FRAME

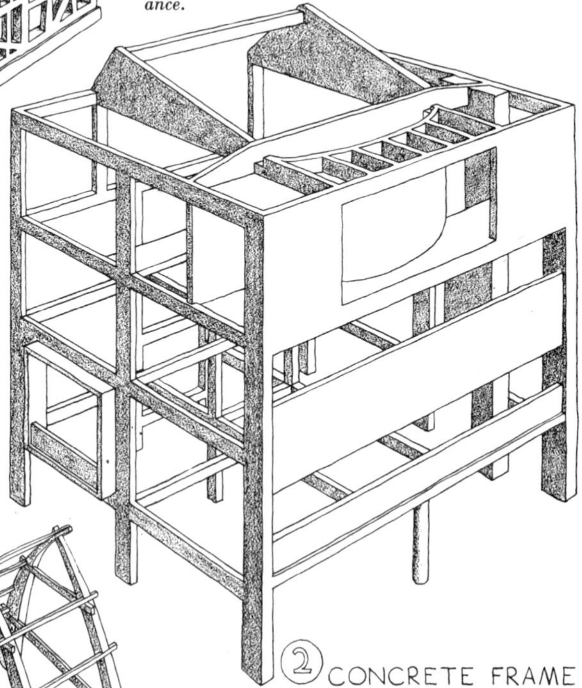

CRUCK

The Peasant's House of pages 12 and 13 is analysed in Fig. 3. The drawing shows all structural members. The whole roof weight is carried to earth by the crucks. The ridge is clearly visible at the apex, and so are the three rows of purlins on each side, and cross ties for uniting the opposing members of the pairs of crucks. The low side walls and ends must only resist the weather and be self-supporting.

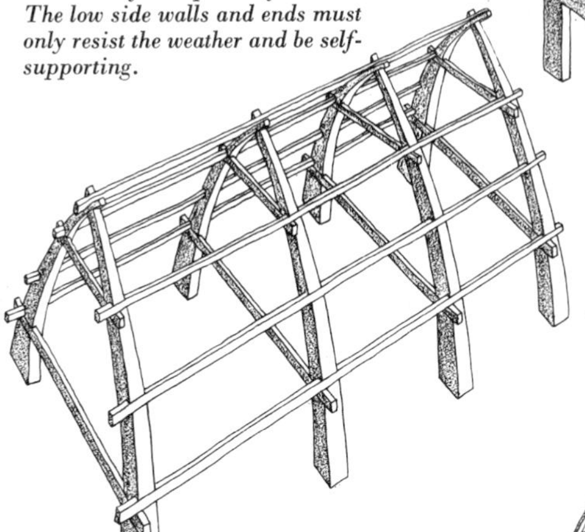

② CONCRETE FRAME.

③ CRUCK

LOAD-BEARING WALL

Here are two examples of the load-bearing wall system. Fig. 4 represents a house built with stone, which is drawn in detail on pages 16 and 17. It has long stone lintels over openings in the walls for carrying the weight over. Fig. 5 is of a brick house. Openings at the higher levels are spanned by flat brick arches (explained Fig. 10, back endpaper) and semi-circular arches on the ground floor. It is an analysis of one of the houses in the crescent on pages 24 and 25. The remaining houses in the book built with the load-bearing wall system are illustrated on the following pages: 4, 5; 8—house letters A, C and D; 9—house letters E and H; 18, 20, 22, 23, 26, 28, 29, 32, 34, 35, 36, 39, 42, and 47.

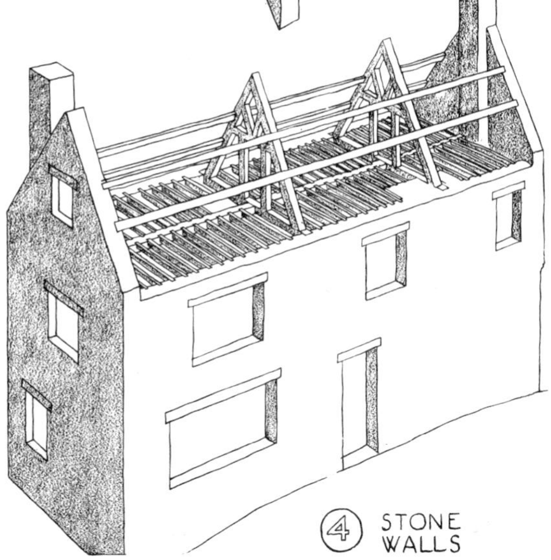

④ STONE WALLS

⑤ BRICK WALLS

A This house is built of hard Derbyshire stone, and belongs to about the same period as the Cotswold house on pages 18 and 19. The stone roofing slabs of the North are larger, hence the flatter roof slopes (explained Fig. 13, back endpaper). The enrichment is more sturdy, carved from the harder stone.

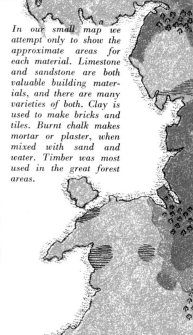

In our small map we attempt only to show the approximate areas for each material. Limestone and sandstone are both valuable building materials, and there are many varieties of both. Clay is used to make bricks and tiles. Burnt chalk makes mortar or plaster, when mixed with sand and water. Timber was most used in the great forest areas.

B In the Welsh border counties of Cheshire, Shropshire, Worcester, and Hereford, large forests led to the widespread use of timber frame construction. The black coloured timbers and white daub panels suggested the name of 'Magpie Style'. It spread along the upper Severn valley across central Wales.

This is a typical Welsh farm-house and buildings, made of rough stone. The custom still is to colourwash walls, sometimes farm and buildings white, frequently the house in pale colour. The roof is covered with purple Welsh slates. Such a house may have been built anytime during the last three hundred years, although thatch was usual in earlier days.

C

This cottage is built of cob, that is mud mixed with straw, bu[ilt] up in stages and allowed to dry out. The garden wall (left) [is] thatched against rain. Cob buildings are most numerous in t[he] south-west. Corners are rounded to prevent cracking.

D

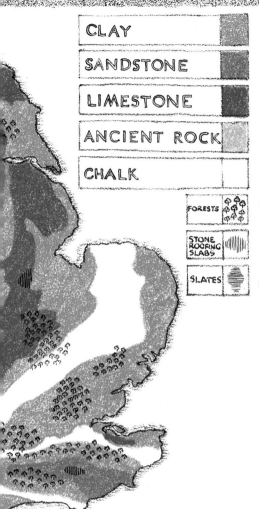

CLAY

SANDSTONE

LIMESTONE

ANCIENT ROCK

CHALK

FORESTS

STONE ROOFING SLABS

SLATES

H *After the Romans left England, bricks and tiles were seldom used until the Fifteenth Century. Some of the earliest of the smaller brick houses exist in east coast towns, often built with Dutch bricks. Features such as the curved or stepped gables are similar to contemporary Dutch buildings.*

G *The two-storied overhanging (or 'jettied') gables, show this house has a timber frame below the plaster, which covers frame and panels alike. This method was common in the eastern counties, where exist also the best examples of patterned plasterwork, called 'pargetting'. The nearer gable is pargetted.*

...his is a Cotswold house. Outside walls were usually low, with ...pper floor within the roof (lit by gables) because the stone walls ...re insufficiently strong for a height of two storeys owing to ...ugh bonding and an absence of inside stone cross walls.

E

The forests of the Home Counties provided plenty of timber for frame construction. Panels were often of plaster and later of brick. Sometimes frame and panel were covered by tile-hanging, or weatherboarding (see Figs. 2 and 3 back endpaper). This house, built about 1750, has a wooden frame. Notice the fashionable details. Many such houses remain in Kent.

F

A 15ᵀᴴ CENTURY

PERSPECTIVE VIEW

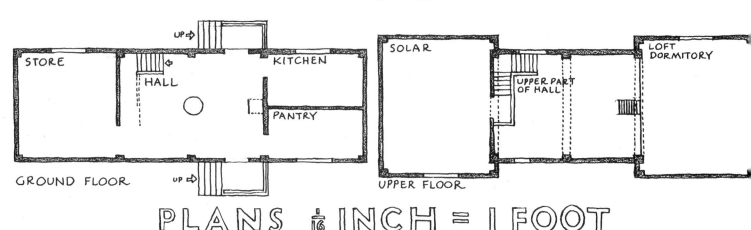

STORE

UP ⇨

KITCHEN

HALL

PANTRY

GROUND FLOOR

UP ⇨

SOLAR

UPPER PART OF HALL

LOFT DORMITORY

UPPER FLOOR

PLANS 1/16 INCH = 1 FOOT

64'

THIS is an example of an early timber-framed building, this particular type being found chiefly in Sussex and the surrounding counties. Wherever timber was the principal building material, houses were built either on this framing method or by use of 'crucks' (see pages 12-13). In districts where stone was plentiful, such as Yorkshire, Lincolnshire and Dorset, stone farmhouses would be found instead of these timbered buildings.

Sheep-farming was paying well during the Fifteenth Century and many of the more prosperous farmers were able to arrange with the Lord of the Manor to make a cash payment for the use of strips of land, thus becoming tenants and ceasing to pay their dues to the lord by working his land for him. Thus arose a new rural middle class living in homes such as this, modelled on the Lord's Manor. Timber was plentiful when these houses were built and the uprights of the frame (or studs) are spaced closely together.

This is a 'Collar Roof'. The 'collars' are the horizontal wooden pieces which span the house, linking each pair of rafters a little above half-way up their length. The main vertical framework for the hall wall consists of six large posts. To keep them steady they are also tied together by three tie beams. Added to their main job, these tie beams carry a shortened form of king post, to support a horizontal member running below the collars. This is not the usual form of roof truss (as defined in front endpaper) which helps to support the roof by carrying purlins. Sprockets have been attached to the feet of the rafters, and this gives an upward curve to the roof at the eaves. Three large brackets are used to support the eaves in front of the hall. Smoke from the central fire escapes through the roof ventilator.

AXONOMETRIC ⅛ INCH = 1 FOOT

0' | | | | | | | | | | | | | | | | | | | | | | | | | | | | | | | | | | | | | | | | | 42'

Let us examine the timber framing more closely. Wherever there are two storeys (that is at each end of the house), the building projects rward about two feet at first floor level. This projection, or overhang, is known as a 'jetty'.

The wall frame for each floor was built separately as follows: a series of upright posts was jointed to a horizontal beam at the bottom—lled the cill—and to another horizontal beam at the top called the head. The joists or floor beams of the upper storey were then rested the head of the lower storey frame, projecting about two feet beyond it; the cill of the upper frame rested on the tops of these joists and acted as ballast weight to steady them. Of course, to keep the balance, the other ends of the joists had either to project as jetties on the her side of the building or pass into heavy cross beams. The central hall ran right up to the roof, without division into storeys.

Wall panels within the structural frame are filled with wattle and clay (see Fig. 1, back endpaper).

A 15TH CENTURY

OUTSIDE PERSPECTIVE

PLAN — 1/16 INCH = 1 FOOT

SECTION — 1/8 INCH = 1 FOOT

HOUSE

SHED

Plan labels: WINDOW, WINDOW, WINDOW, LOOSE BOX, SPACE FOR 3 COWS, CRUCK OVER, SPACE FOR 2 OXEN, ANIMAL FOOD STORE, CRUCK OVER, FIRE, LIVING ROOM, CALF BOX, DOOR, WINDOW, WINDOW, DOOR, WINDOW, ROW OF POLES CARRYING FLOOR OVER, ROW OF POLES CARRYING FLOOR OVER, CRUCK OVER, CRUCK OVER

SHED

The walls of shed and house alike bear no weight. But the method of supporting the ridge-piece varies. For long buildings crucks would give the advantage of clear floor space, uninterrupted by posts.

The chimney was omitted from the section of the house in favour of showing the normal roof construction, with thatch lapped at the ridge, and the extra thickness. The section is taken through the Living Room, looking towards the animals' quarters. A ladder gives access to the loft, and the poles forming the loft floor are showing. The door is behind the kneeling woman.

THIS house is constructed with crucks, a method which was used mainly in the north of England, Scotland and Wales. Crucks are larg curved beams, arranged in opposing pairs, with their foundations on stone or on the ground, and their tops meeting at the roof ape rather like the framework of an upturned boat. The weight of the roof is transferred to the crucks by beams, called 'purlins', running t length of the building. The low side walls simply keep out the weather. Crucks with a good bend gave the best head-room near the side wal but they would still compare unfavourably with the vertical walls of the framing method. Moreover, the width of the house was limited l the size of cruck available, and it was impossible to have an upper floor except in the roof itself.

The normal Open Field system was never widely adopted in Wales and the North, and there were many peasant farmers who would li with their animals in houses like this one.

AXONOMETRIC ⅛INCH = 1 FOOT

Four pairs of crucks have been used in this house, secured at the apex and with horizontal beams tying them together. The house place, single room, open to the roof, with central fire and roof-hole for the smoke, occupies one-third of the building. The remainder is given ver to the animals and has a loft above (omitted from the axonometric to show more clearly how the space beneath is divided). The lower e-beams and the cross poles above the mangers would easily have supported a loft floor of poles, which would be useful for hay storage d would make a warm and comfortable sleeping place. For the side walls there is a double row of wooden stakes, interwoven with wattles, e space between packed with mud. The mud would outlast the wattles, particularly if reinforced with straw. (Such walls are known as ob'.) The roof is thatched with reeds on 'flaking', which is an undercoat of woven reeds laid across the rafters to form a level bed.

A 16TH CENTURY C

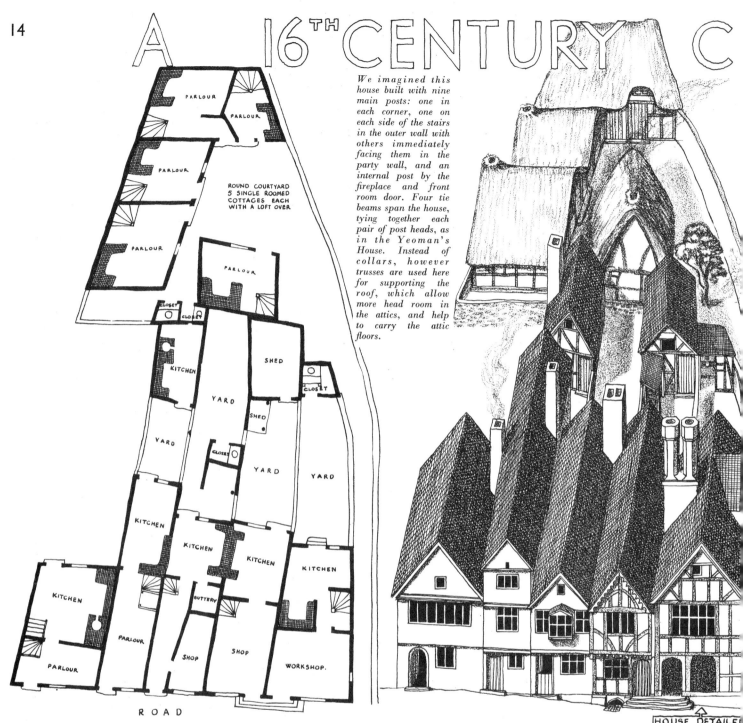

Labels in plan: PARLOUR, PARLOUR, PARLOUR, PARLOUR, PARLOUR, PARLOUR, ROUND COURTYARD 5 SINGLE ROOMED COTTAGES EACH WITH A LOFT OVER, CLOSET, CLOSET, KITCHEN, SHED, YARD, CLOSET, SHED, YARD, CLOSET, YARD, YARD, KITCHEN, KITCHEN, KITCHEN, KITCHEN, KITCHEN, BUTTERY, PARLOUR, SHOP, SHOP, WORKSHOP, PARLOUR, ROAD, HOUSE DETAILED

We imagined this house built with nine main posts: one in each corner, one on each side of the stairs in the outer wall with others immediately facing them in the party wall, and an internal post by the fireplace and front room door. Four tie beams span the house, tying together each pair of post heads, as in the Yeoman's House. Instead of collars, however trusses are used here for supporting the roof, which allow more head room in the attics, and help to carry the attic floors.

PLAN & AXONOMETRIC OF PART OF A TOWN – SCALE $\frac{1^{IN}}{16}$ =

WE turn now to a town house, one of the kind built in the Sixteenth Century when town populations were increasing. It is a timber-frame two storeyed house, but has vertical walls without jetties, like the hall part of the Yeoman's house on pages 10 and 11. When, in the Sixteenth Century, houses came to have chimneys and staircases, a system of framing was used in upper floors which made jetties unnecessary except in tall buildings. To save timber, which was becoming scarce, framing panels were made larger and stiffened with cross-pieces at angles, where extra strength was required.

In the Sixteenth Century, town houses usually possessed gardens or yards, and generally speaking it was not until much later that these open spaces were taken for building sites. The streets were narrow and crooked, but this was not a great inconvenience when there was little or no wheeled traffic. Our drawing shows part of a town based on plans of London published in 1612. Five old-type houses are grouped round a courtyard at the back and, along the road, new houses and shops have been built on the odd-shaped sites of earlier ones. The latest developments are here—tiles, inside chimneys, and big windows. As soon as glass was available, timber-framed houses had rows of windows, because it was as easy to fill panels with glass as with plaster.

The corner house next to the passage is detailed on the opposite page. There is a bootmakers' shop and a kitchen on the ground floor, two rooms for the master and family upstairs, and servants' and apprentices' quarters under the roof. The principal room on the first floor has wooden panels lining the walls, enriched with 'linenfold' pattern. (Damp and cold would penetrate particularly through the joint between the frame and the infilling, and wood panelling was a useful protection.) The stone fireplace has a flat Tudor arch, and the bay window has five lights divided by mullions and transomes. Glass could only be made in small pieces, which were joined with strips of lead and fixed in an iron frame.

To allow the best living room to appear on the isometric, the attic floor above has been removed, and the walls and roof cut away the better to demonstrate the building. Bricks were still uncommon, and if they had been used for infilling the panels (which gradually became the practice in clay districts) the owners would probably have been too proud to have covered the bricks with a coat of plaster, as we have shown. When plaster is used it is commonly taken over the frame and panel alike in order to waterproof the joint. A small gable has been provided to accommodate the top stairs.

DETAILED ISOMETRIC
SCALE $\frac{1}{4}$ INCH = 1 FOOT

The nearest tiler is trimming the imperfect edges and projections from stone roofing slabs. Lying on the ground close beside him is the tool used for holing the slabs. For piercing, the slab will again be held against the metal edge, and given a sharp tap with the pointed end of the tool. After holing, the slabs are measured and separated into groups of similar sized slabs, ready for hanging by wooden pegs from battens which cross the rafters.

THE Seventeenth Century saw the building of new farmhouses in many parts of the country, because food production was becoming mor important, and large sheep-runs would be split into several farms of arable, requiring additional farmhouses. In wooded districts timbe continued to be used in the old way, though more sparingly, and occasionally, as bricks became more plentiful, the ground floor of timber building would be rebuilt in brickwork (and in other cases, stone) to the underside of the jetty. Many houses with this alteratio still exist. In stone districts load-bearing walls were already the rule. The Cotswold area is one such, where Seventeenth Century prosperit in farming is reflected in the number and excellence of buildings surviving, one of which serves here as an example of stone constructio

In timber buildings the roof weight is transferred to the ground only at certain points, whether by crucks or by the posts in a frame Load-bearing walls, of brick or stone, are on a completely different principle, and bear the weight throughout their whole length, thei strength depending upon the stones or bricks fitting well together (their 'bonding'). Walls built with rough, 'undressed' stones are weak an must be thick, but dressed stones may be made into a thinner wall. In this house, the stones are roughly dressed to allow the jointing t be horizontal, or 'coursed'. Stone slabs, or lintels, span door and window openings, the widths being limited by the size of lintel stone available. The men in the right of the picture are sorting and trimming the thin stone slabs used for roofing. The larger slabs were used a the eaves, the smaller at the ridge. In Derbyshire and Yorkshire, also stone districts, the roofing slabs are larger and the roofs flatter. Fulle details of stone walls are given in Fig. 11 and of roof pitches in Fig. 13 of the back endpaper.

STORE

BEDROOM | EXISTING PARTITIONS | BEDROOM

1ST FLOOR 1/32"=1'.

DOWN | ATTIC | ATTIC | ATTIC

ATTICS 1/32"=1'.

UP

PARLOUR

KITCHEN | FOOD STORE

BREAD OVEN

GROUND FLOOR PLAN SCALE 1/16"=1'. 0' 10'

ISOMETRIC SCALE 1/8"=1'.

0' 16'

This particular house was built in 1618, and remains almost unchanged except for the addition of a storey on the back wing, which we have omitted in our drawing. In these early solid-wall houses, craftsmen settled the positions of windows, doors and chimneys from their traditional knowledge of local materials and building practice. A comparison between this building, which shows no Renaissance influence, and the two that follow will give some idea of the changes that took place in house-building as the century progressed.

The usual plan for a small farmhouse of this period has the kitchen and parlour end to end, sharing a common chimney-stack, with sometimes an additional parlour reached through the first. Staircases were often tucked in beside the chimney-stack, and extensions were frequently made at the sides to provide extra rooms, either by continuing the roof slope to form a cat-slide (see front endpaper), or by building out short wings, as is the case here.

The upright stones ('mullions') in each window give extra support to the lintels, and the mouldings above the windows are known as 'drip moulds' because it is their job to make the rain-water drip clear of the opening. All the enrichment of this house is confined to a few structural members—the entrance door arch stones, the drip moulds and mullions, the chimney cappings, etc. This serves to emphasize the form and construction of the house.

Part of the roof and upper floor and walls have been removed on the isometric drawing to show clearly the construction and arrangement of space. Two trusses support the roof purlins, and the first floor joists span from the outer walls to central beams running lengthways. These in turn are carried by two cross beams and the end walls.

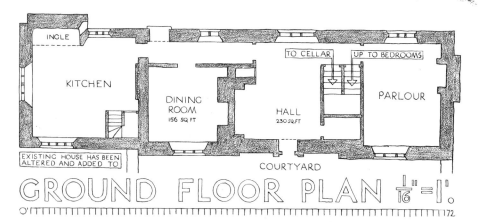

INGLE

KITCHEN

TO CELLAR · UP TO BEDROOMS

DINING ROOM 156 SQ FT

HALL 230 SQ FT

PARLOUR

EXISTING HOUSE HAS BEEN ALTERED AND ADDED TO

COURTYARD

GROUND FLOOR PLAN 1/16"=1'.

THE influence of the Renaissance on architectu[re] in England can be traced from the middle of t[he] Sixteenth Century, when builders discovered the works of antiquity a grammar and logic ornament which they had previously lacked. I[n] other words they discovered the art of arch[i]tecture. This led gradually to the fashion f[or] designing buildings and towns as architectur[al] compositions. Thus, the element of fashion building style becomes an important consider[a]tion. Prior to this, 'following the fashion' seem[s] to have been largely a matter of fitting in t[he] latest development in construction or househo[ld] comfort, whether a large glazed window, woo[d] panelling or a new inside chimney.

The new ideas were imported from Italy, where it was already he fashion to copy buildings of the old classical pattern, based on he principle of symmetry or balance, and ornamented in the style f the ruins of ancient Rome and Greece, and the first result of an pplication of those rules was a great tidying-up of the outsides f buildings. As time went on, architects became more inclined ierely to copy classical models, and their work was more imitative han inspired.

We have stressed the close connection between form and con-truction, and it is obvious from the materials used and the hand-ng of the openings of the house drawn here that it is constructed ith weight-carrying walls on similar lines to the farmhouse on ages 16 and 17. But there are differences in window, door and himney pattern, and in ornamentation. The farmhouse is pre-Renaissance, this house is influenced by the Renaissance fashion,

but only to a limited degree. Most obvious is the front door, in the centre of the main front, with the windows arranged symmetrically on either hand, and the balance stressed by the semi-circular rise in the wall over the middle window (called a pediment), and the hipped roof. Ornamentation (the door, for instance, and the eaves cornice) is freely inspired by classical models. But whereas Renaissance builders came to favour the sash-window because it was more adaptable to classical proportions, this house has the old type, similar to the farmhouse windows except that, being larger, they have a transome for extra strength. The plan also, with its large central hall, is in the old tradition, and the hall chimney goes straight up through the roof, ignoring symmetrical effect. This house is an interesting example because it shows how local builders in out-of-the-way places, while incorporating new ideas from London and abroad, retained what they wished of the old tradition.

ENTRANCE DETAIL

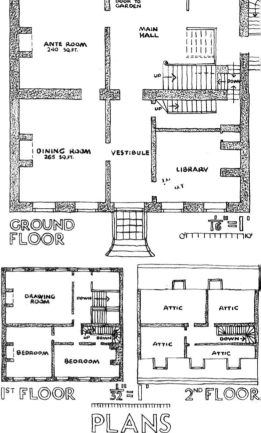

DOOR TO GARDEN

MAIN HALL

ANTE ROOM
240 SQ.FT.

UP

DOWN

UP

DINING ROOM
265 SQ.FT.

VESTIBULE

LIBRARY

GROUND FLOOR

$\frac{1}{16}'' = 1'$

DRAWING ROOM

DOWN

BEDROOM

UP DOWN

BEDROOM

ATTIC

ATTIC

ATTIC

DOWN

ATTIC

1ST FLOOR

$\frac{1}{32}'' = 1'$

2ND FLOOR

PLANS

AS we have already described, architects workin
in the classical style have generally preferred
solid wall. Timber was becoming increasingl
scarce, and this, together with the fear of fir
(following the fire of London), was another reaso
for increased use of brick. From being the excep
tion, solid weight-carrying walls became the rul

The Later Renaissance period of Englis
Architecture is usually regarded as a golden age o
taste. It was a taste popularized by the land
owning class who, through the security of wealt
and consequent leisure, were able to develo
discernment in the arts to a degree since un
equalled.

The house illustrated is modelled on one buil
on the outskirts of London about 1700. It is
brick house, designed on the classical princip
of symmetry, with classical details and sash
windows. As no new principles of construction ar
involved, we have set out to show proportion
and detail, giving a perspective of the outsid
and another of the entrance doorway to a large
scale. Notice with what restraint the Classica
enrichments are used, and compare with th
richly ornate Victorian house on page 29. Th
bold cornice of timber (typical of late Seventeenth
and early Eighteenth-century domestic work)
painted white; the patterning of the whi
windows with their broad frames contrasts wit
the deep red brick-work; the graceful hood on i
carved brackets and the wrought iron railings ad
dignity to the entrance. Glass could now be mad
in larger panes, and the old lead strips have give
place to broad wooden bars.

KITCHEN LARDER UP WINE STORE UP

BASEMENT

ATTIC ATTIC DRAWING RM. BEDROOM MAIN HALL VESTIBULE KITCHEN

CROSS SECTION

$\frac{1}{32}'' = 1'$

PERSPECTIVE VIEW

Renaissance influence did not affect only exteriors. A glance at the plan of this house will show that it has been divided into regular shapes, matching the orderliness of the elevation. The front door leads into a hall, reduced to vestibule size, with rooms balanced on each side, and then to the staircase hall. To preserve the neat plan, the servants' kitchen has been dug out of the basement and a secondary staircase ingeniously contrived to link it with the attics where the servants slept.

Renaissance architects developed the double span roof so that houses could be two or more rooms deep instead of one. The little section shows how this was done by taking a central load bearing wall up to take the weight from the two inner pitches of the roofs.

Compare the wall thicknesses of this house and that on page 17. These brick walls are much thinner, because bricks are small and precisely uniform in size and shape, and can be strongly bonded into one another. Walls of a single brick thickness (9 inches) are sufficiently strong, and many houses are made of them. This house is very well built, having ground floor external walls two bricks thick, and upstairs walls one and a half bricks thick.

It was not until the Nineteenth Century that much attention was paid to sanitation. In 1700 and for many years afterwards there were no baths in our sense of the word, no water-closets, no sewers and no public water supplies. Water came from a pump, or was caught from the roof in lead rain-water cisterns (many of which were richly patterned). For sewage there was an outside closet with pit—with the consequent risk of pollution of well-water.

We introduced on page 18 the subject of fashions in building. The desire to follow fashions in the appearance and ornamentation of houses would seem to be irresistible, and the worst outcome can only be that our homes will soon appear out of fashion; they will, if history is a reliable guide, return to favour some hundred years later. But change of structural method and building materials is another matter, and careful consideration is required when making a choice, as all change is claimed by somebody as improvement.

INSIDE AN INCONVENIENT UNHEALTHY HOUSE

IN spite of some land enclosure the Midland areas of England were mainly farmed, until the Eighteenth Century, on the old Open Field system, which had been used in Saxon times to give everyone a few strips of land for cultivation and use of the commons for pasture. When, in the Eighteenth Century, more efficient ploughs, seed drills, and other inventions and new methods came into use, it was found that bigger farms were much more easily and profitably worked than the narrow strips of land. By the Enclosure Acts, Parliament made it possible for strips to be joined, common land to be taken over, and large farms set up. This dispossessed many small-holders and they either migrated to towns or became labourers on the large farms. Most of them lived in poor hovels and would have thought themselves lucky to have so good a house as the one shown here.

Our drawing is a reconstruction based upon the remains of several old cottages, inhabited until the late 1930's, sufficiently primitive in construction and plan to serve our purpose. Fortunately we were able to gain additional information from a report we came across, written by an architect named John Wood in 1777 and containing descriptions of houses of this type. It appears that labourers' houses were in such a ruinous state at this time that some landlords employed their architects to design new cottages for the workers on their estates. 'Early in the summer of 1777,' writes John Wood, 'I was in the company of some four gentlemen of landed property when the conversation turned on the ruinous state of the cottages of this kingdom; it was observed that these habitations of that useful and necessary rank of men, the labourers, were become for the most part offensive both to decency and humanity.' He decided to investigate, and these are some of his findings. Because walls were too thin, water came through joints, and it was so cold in some cottages that ice formed over inside walls: damp was caused by leaky roofs and badly-fitting doors, and by the practice of building into hillsides and below ground level; there were many cottages without ceilings, with holes in the roof, or with draughts blowing through doors which opened directly into living rooms. One of the worst features, as it still is to-day, was the overcrowding. 'It is melancholy,' he says, 'to see a man, his wife and half a dozen children crowded together in the same room, nay, often into the same bed; the horror is still heightened and the inconvenience increased at the time when the women is in child-bed, or in case of illness or death.' After making his report John Wood suggested better ways of building, and published a series of designs, one of which is shown on the opposite page.

It was many years, however, before the public took any real interest in the provision of healthier and better houses. A notable advance was made in 1875, when the Public Health Act resulted in the setting up of building by-laws under which plans and construction of any new building had to be approved by local councils before work could commence. No real progress was made in the struggle against overcrowding until after the 1914-18 war; and as a result of the Second World War the position did not improve for some time.

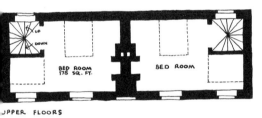

BED ROOM 175 SQ. FT.

BED ROOM

UPPER FLOORS

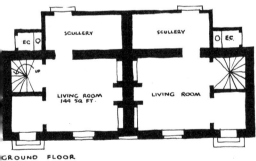

SCULLERY

SCULLERY

E.C.

E.C.

LIVING ROOM 144 SQ. FT.

LIVING ROOM

GROUND FLOOR

SCALE ⅛" = 1' 0' 132'

ARCHITECTS DESIGN

These houses have sash windows, then the commonest type. Openings for windows and doors are spanned by segmental arches of ordinary bricks, with those surrounding cut to fit. The flat arch used for the windows of the house on pages 20 and 21 would be made of specially moulded bricks. The left-hand plan has thicker walls for stone construction, while those on the right are brick—thirteen and a half inches on the ground floor and nine inches above.

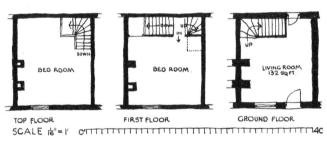

BED ROOM

BED ROOM

UP IN

LIVING ROOM 132 SQ FT.

TOP FLOOR

FIRST FLOOR

GROUND FLOOR

SCALE ⅛"=1' 0'

HOUSES PLANNED FOR MILL WORKERS

For the roof of the house opposite we show a method of thatching we have seen on one or two old cottages. The thatch is straw, not reeds as described on page 13, and to get some sort of level bed above the rough branches, straw ropes were used as flaking. They were about 1½ inches thick, made of twisted straw, and passed from ridge to eaves. When eventually they rotted they hung down in festoons. Two hundred years ago briars would probably have been used to hold down the thatch. A more recent method makes use of wooden battens nailed across the rafters to form a bed, and the thatch held down by tarred string (see Figs. 15 and 16 of back endpaper).

There were other inventions at this time in addition to the improved farm machinery: early in the century came new machines for spinning and weaving wool in place of the old spinning wheel and hand loom. To house them, mills were built, and as the early mills were driven by water-power, they were erected near the streams, where accommodation for workers would be difficult to find. The drawing on this page shows a group of cottages built by a mill-owner to accommodate his workers, a part of a larger but rather haphazardly planned scheme. We show the cottages as they were when first built, omitting the extra rooms added at the rear at a later date. The brick faces with their white painted sash-windows remain little changed.

We chose these houses because of their similarity in plan to the architect's model house of 1777 and the later city houses of the Industrial Revolution shown on page 28, with which they make a link. They illustrate well the difference that lay-out makes: though similar in plan these early industrial villages retained their orchards and gardens, and the open country was close at hand: in the Nineteenth Century cities, on the other hand, congestion was so great that the houses were built back to back round courts.

LATE 18TH CENTUR

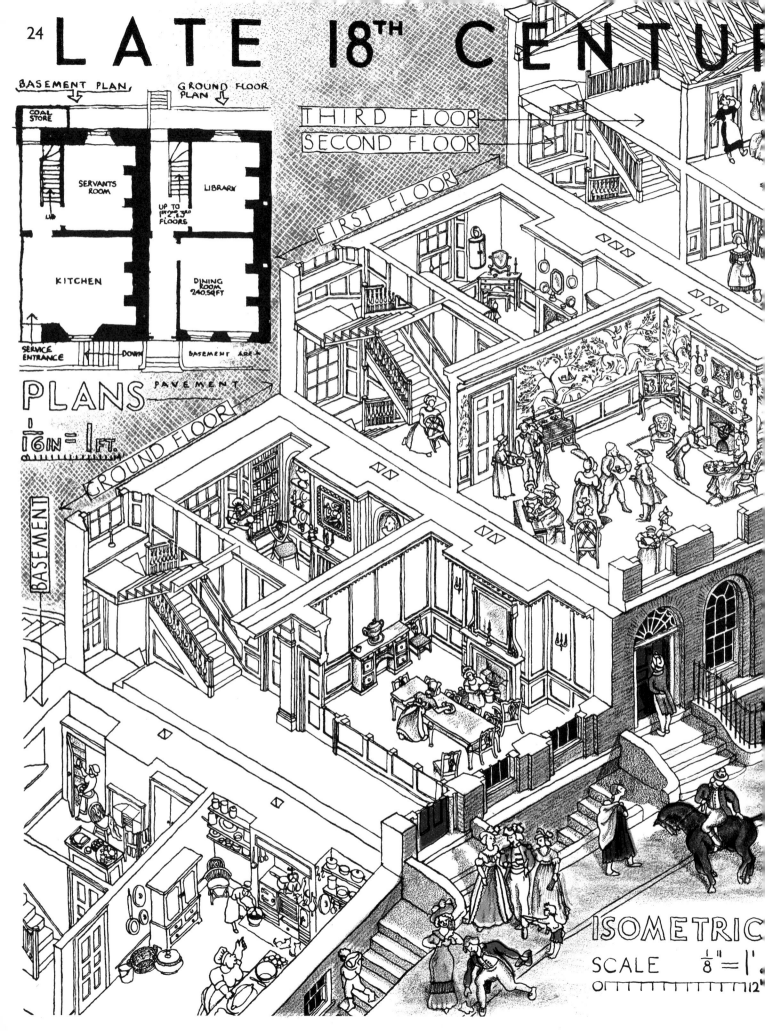

BASEMENT PLAN

GROUND FLOOR PLAN

COAL STORE

SERVANTS ROOM

LWD

LIBRARY

UP TO UPPER 3RD & E. FLOORS

KITCHEN

DINING ROOM 240.SQ.FT

SERVICE ENTRANCE

DOWN

BASEMENT AREA

PLANS

PAVEMENT

$\frac{1}{16}$IN = 1 FT.

THIRD FLOOR

SECOND FLOOR

FIRST FLOOR

GROUND FLOOR

BASEMENT

ISOMETRIC

SCALE $\frac{1}{8}$" = 1'

0   12

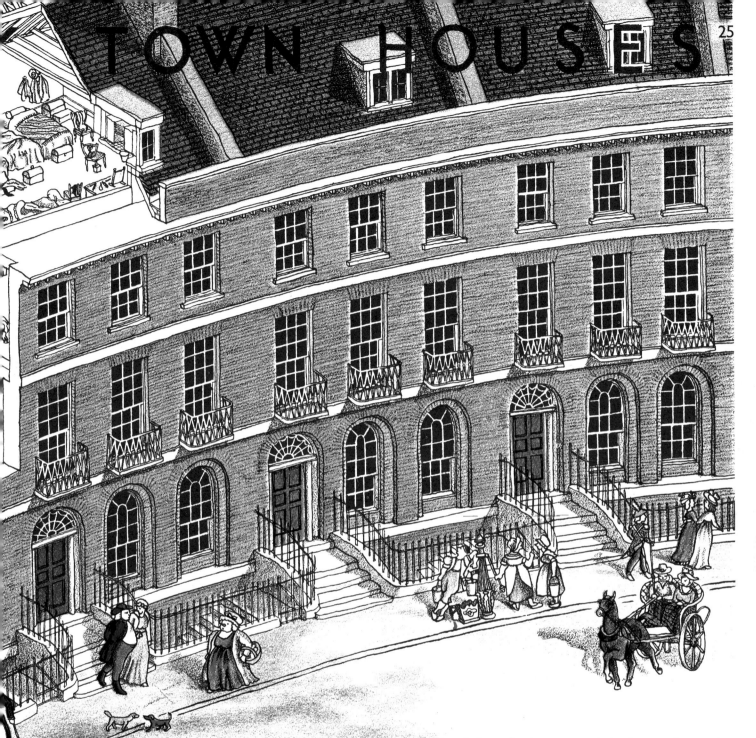

ᴡᴇ have described how the mediæval town grew up, with houses becoming crowded together in narrow twisting lanes, quite unsuitable for dashing carriages. We must now consider how the Eighteenth-century town houses, with their load-bearing walls and tidy appearance, were often joined to form terraces. You will notice that the houses on this page are designed to form part of a crescent (the remainder of which is shown on page 27). In other words, they are designed as a unit, unlike the haphazard growth of mediæval towns, and unlike some of our Twentieth-century houses, which appear to express a desire to be different from everybody else. As the drawing shows, the unity has been carefully emphasized by continuous bands of enrichment in the form of cornice, and stone bands, or 'string courses'.

Our reconstruction is based on a study of the County of London Surveys, and shows typical late Eighteenth-century medium-sized town houses. Plans were uniform, varying only a few feet in width, but the poorer houses had only two storeys, while the larger ones had three or four, with attics in the roof, and kitchens usually built into the basement—an arrangement that served well enough as long as servants could be found to do the running about.

Although panelling was no longer required to keep out the damp and draught, it remained in fashion in a simplified form with larger panels. It was soon to be replaced, however, in popular taste by plaster and wall-paper. Following extensions of our Far East trade, a Chinese fashion made its appearance about 1760, and Chinese wall-papers were imported and enthusiastically received. Hence the Chinese wall-paper, with furnishings to match, in our first floor front room.

For those who are interested in identifying the age of a building, it is useful to notice that houses of this period vary in several details from those built about a hundred years earlier. Sash windows came to be set back from the outer brick wall-face, the frames being hidden in a brick recess. Glazing bars were reduced in width, cornices were smaller if not omitted altogether, and a parapet commonly hid the roof. (Compare these houses with that on pages 20 and 21.) Sanitary conveniences remained little changed, however, and public pumps still supplied the drinking water.

A REGENCY HOUSE

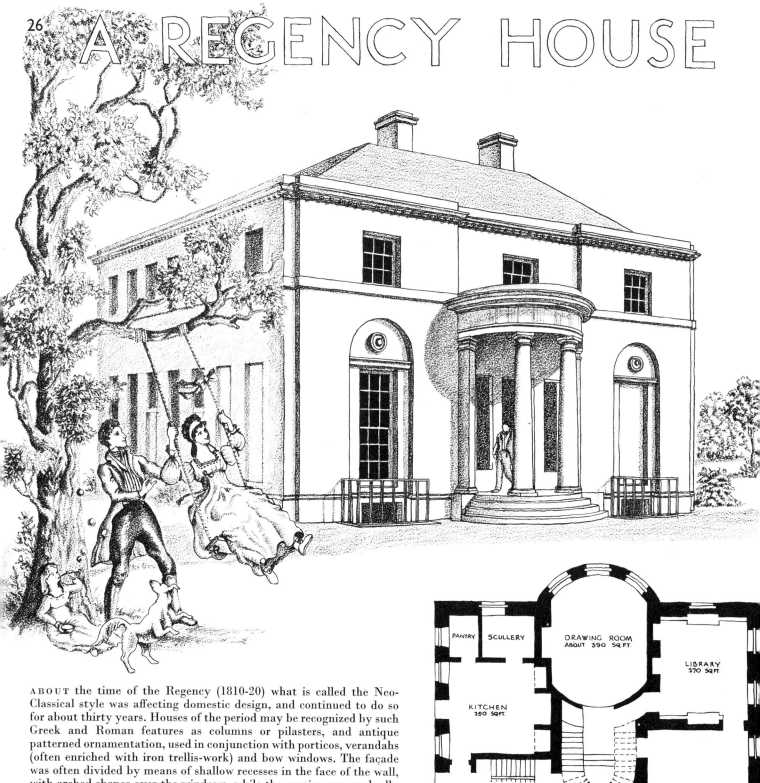

ABOUT the time of the Regency (1810-20) what is called the Neo-Classical style was affecting domestic design, and continued to do so for about thirty years. Houses of the period may be recognized by such Greek and Roman features as columns or pilasters, and antique patterned ornamentation, used in conjunction with porticos, verandahs (often enriched with iron trellis-work) and bow windows. The façade was often divided by means of shallow recesses in the face of the wall, with arched shapes over the windows, while the cornice was gradually reduced in size and gave place to overhanging eaves.

Medium-sized houses built in Neo-Classical style are fairly common. They were in demand for the new professional classes who wanted a home in the suburbs, and North London, for instance, has many. Since the Nineteenth Century also saw the rise to popularity of the seaside resort and inland spa, such places as Brighton, Scarborough and Cheltenham contain many examples.

The house on this page, with its entrance portico complete with columns, represents the period for us. The plan shows the extent to which architects had adopted the principle of plan-patterning, a style which was mainly popularized by the Adam brothers, and continued in favour to the end of the Regency.

By 1850 the Neo-Classical style had dropped out of fashion on account of popular desire for a change. The garden designed on a geometrical principle was the first part of the scheme to change, giving place to the natural garden.

PANTRY SCULLERY

DRAWING ROOM
ABOUT 390 SQ.FT.

LIBRARY
270 SQ.FT.

KITCHEN
250 SQ.FT.

EATING ROOM
450 SQ.FT.

BREAKFAST ROOM
230 SQ.FT.

HALL

GROUND FLOOR

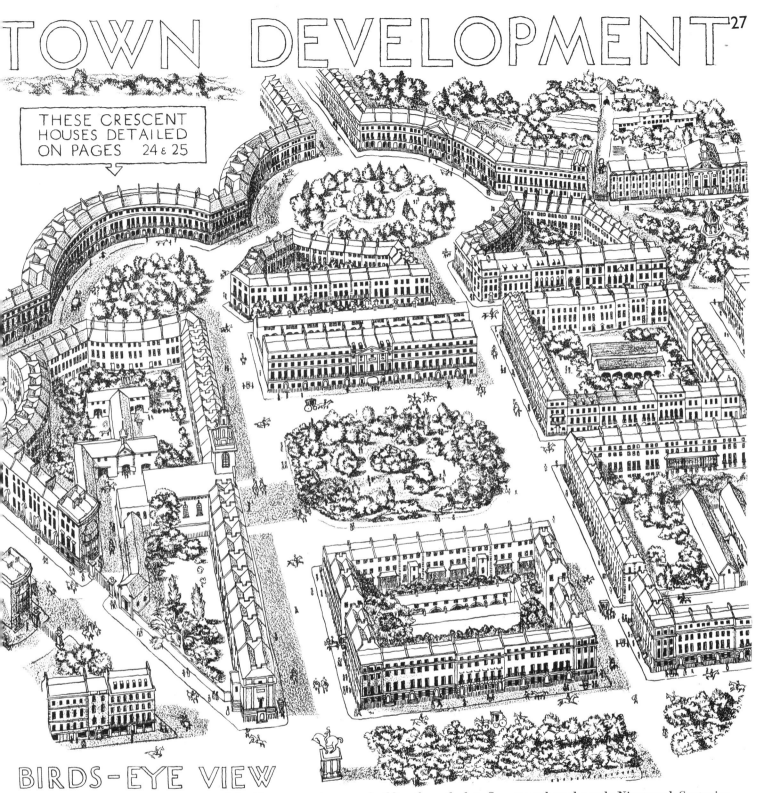

THESE CRESCENT HOUSES DETAILED ON PAGES 24 & 25

BIRDS-EYE VIEW

This picture attempts to set out some of the ideas governing town building from the late Seventeenth to the early Nineteenth Centuries. Houses are neatly grouped together to form streets, squares, crescents and circuses. Trees play a large and agreeable part in the scheme, but they are never allowed to interfere with the grouping of the houses. The streets, to anyone walking through them, are unmistakably those of a town. It was not till later, when squalid industrial cities had sprung up, that the need was felt to disguise new towns as countryside.

The idea of terraced houses (i.e. attached houses) became unpopular in England because of the way the Victorians mishandled it. They built their terraces into monotonous, equally-spaced streets, and they spoiled the unity by breaking up their wall faces with projecting bay-windows and with misplaced ornamentation, and their roofs with clumsy chimneys. Add to this that, being intended mainly for workers, these terraces were built close to factories, and you will appreciate why a reaction took place against the terraced house in favour of winding streets (christened 'drives' or 'avenues') and semi-detached grandeur.

Notice in contrast how pleasantly the Georgian builders arranged their houses and how their ornamentation was used to emphasize the unity of the streets. Most of this development was speculative building, just as it has been during most of this century. But the Georgians, even when they let off individual plots to small builders, always employed an architect surveyor who supervised the scheme: window patterns, the height of cornice and horizontal bands, were all dictated. To-day, dictation sometimes comes indirectly from the public, when councils approve schemes likely to please the electors. Often, however, communications between councils and electors are poor and the public is not in a position to exercise power. It is also true that many people have not had the leisure or the education to enable them to discriminate between good and bad architecture. But increasing interest shows that we are beginning to shoulder our responsibilities.

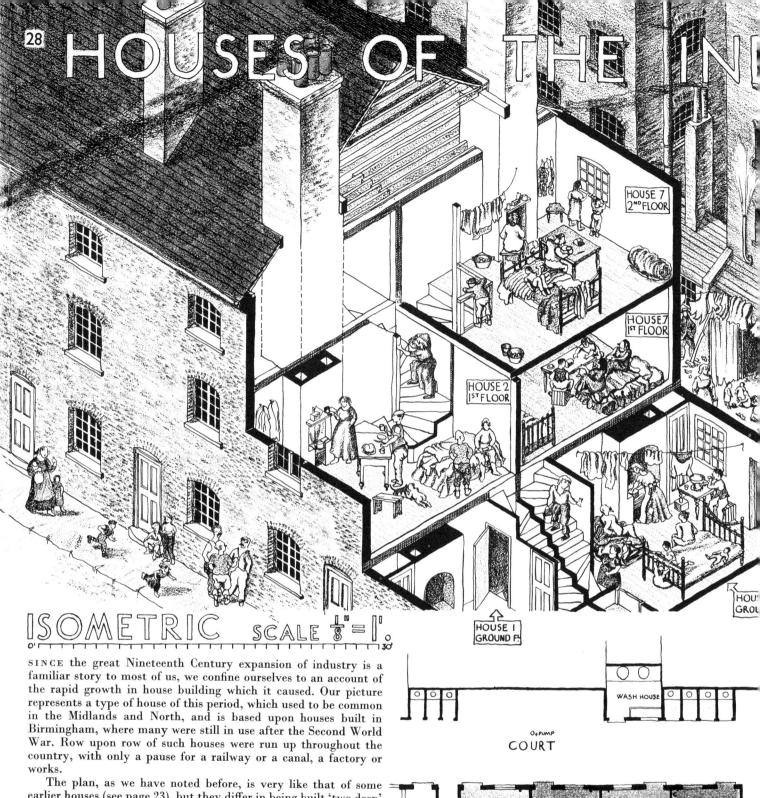

HOUSE 7 2ND FLOOR

HOUSE 7 1ST FLOOR

HOUSE 2 1ST FLOOR

HOUS GROU

HOUSE 1 GROUND F.

ISOMETRIC SCALE ⅛" = 1'.

0' 30

SINCE the great Nineteenth Century expansion of industry is a familiar story to most of us, we confine ourselves to an account of the rapid growth in house building which it caused. Our picture represents a type of house of this period, which used to be common in the Midlands and North, and is based upon houses built in Birmingham, where many were still in use after the Second World War. Row upon row of such houses were run up throughout the country, with only a pause for a railway or a canal, a factory or works.

The plan, as we have noted before, is very like that of some earlier houses (see page 23), but they differ in being built 'two deep' and having no separate closet. The closets and the pump are in a back courtyard round which the houses are grouped, thus involving a long and difficult journey from some of them. The most unpleasant thing about them is not, of course, their back-to-back arrangement, but the absence of bathrooms, kitchens and proper food-storage facilities, and the disagreeable and crowded layouts.

Houses of this sort would now be ranked as slums, and local authorities have pulled down most, if not all, of them. Some were improved by the installation of water-closets in the yards, taps in the houses, and gas or electricity services. In spite of such improvements up to 1939 living conditions in central areas of industrial towns remained generally unsatisfactory, on account of the problems involved in re-planning and re-building large areas. The post-war years saw great strides made (often necessitated by war-time bombing) towards the creation of healthier and more pleasant urban surroundings.

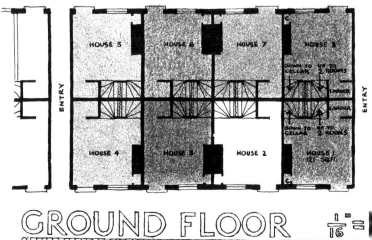

WASH HOUSE

O & PUMP

COURT

ENTRY

HOUSE 5   HOUSE 6   HOUSE 7   HOUSE 8

HOUSE 4   HOUSE 3   HOUSE 2   HOUSE 1 121 SQ.FT.

ENTRY

GROUND FLOOR

⅟₁₆

0'

ROUND FLOOR

CONSERVATORY

PANTRY

KITCHEN
195 SQ FT.

SCULLERY S

UP DOWN

←COPPER

STORE

DRAWING ROOM
350 SQ FT.

STORE

W.C.

DINING ROOM
400 SQ FT.

BREAKFAST
ROOM 180 SQ'

1" = 1'
16

60'

OUTSIDE PERSPECTIVE

When, as far back as the Eighteenth Century, bricks and tiles became fashionable over most of the country, and city architects were employed to design cottages in remote parts, the old habit of building from the materials nearest to hand received a check. By the mid-Nineteenth Century it was often actually cheaper to import materials into a district by rail or canal than to use the local ones.

A house such as the one on this page might have been built almost anywhere in the British Isles about the year 1860. It is of the suburban type, for the suburbs sprang up when railways could both transport the building materials required and also carry the more well-to-do business men daily from outlying districts to their work in the cities. It is built in a modified Gothic style, another variant of which had been employed to a limited extent during the Eighteenth Century for building and furniture. It stands in its own grounds, with great rooms for a multiplicity of functions, needing a huge staff of servants to run it.

The opened-up drawings on the early pages of our book showed changes of construction on almost every page, but these changes stopped at the Renaissance when English builders took to the load-bearing wall, which remains in use to the present day. Although new machine methods were invented in the Nineteenth Century they were not applied to house building, and the opened-up drawing of this house, shown on pages 30 and 31, reflects no new constructional method. It will be noticed that the ground floor, except for the kitchens, is raised on a grassy pedestal for effect. This results in the ill-lit and awkward steps linking service to living quarters (see page 30).

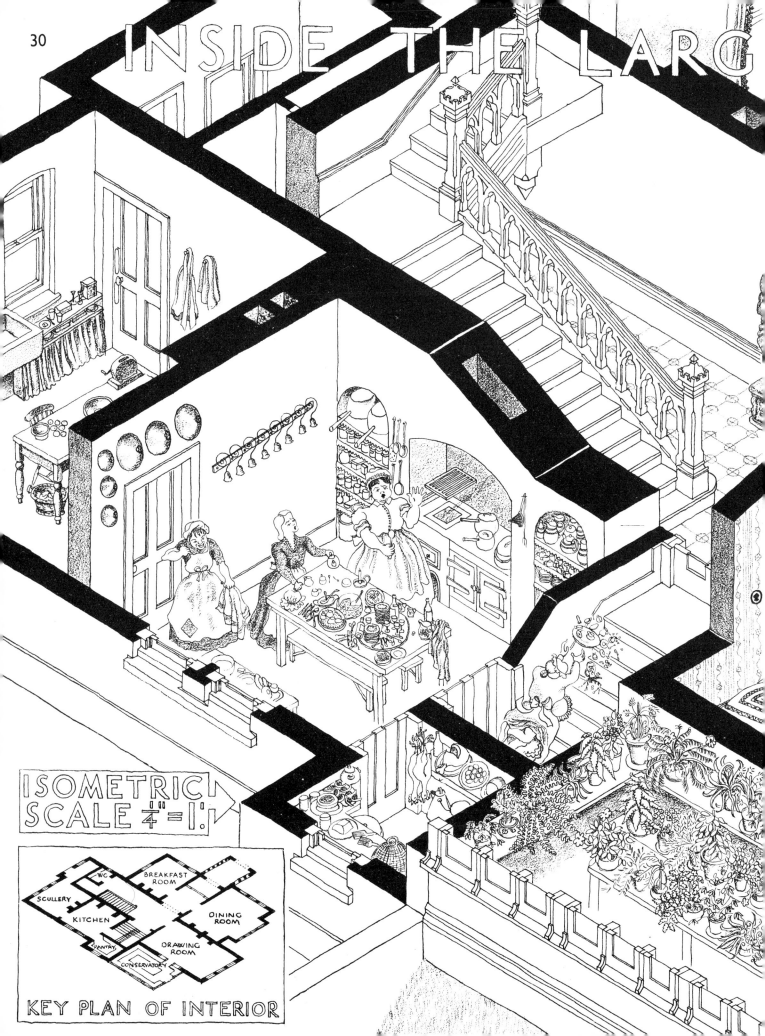

ISOMETRIC
SCALE ¼" = 1'.

WC
BREAKFAST
ROOM
SCULLERY
KITCHEN
DINING
ROOM
PANTRY
DRAWING
ROOM
CONSERVATORY

KEY PLAN OF INTERIOR

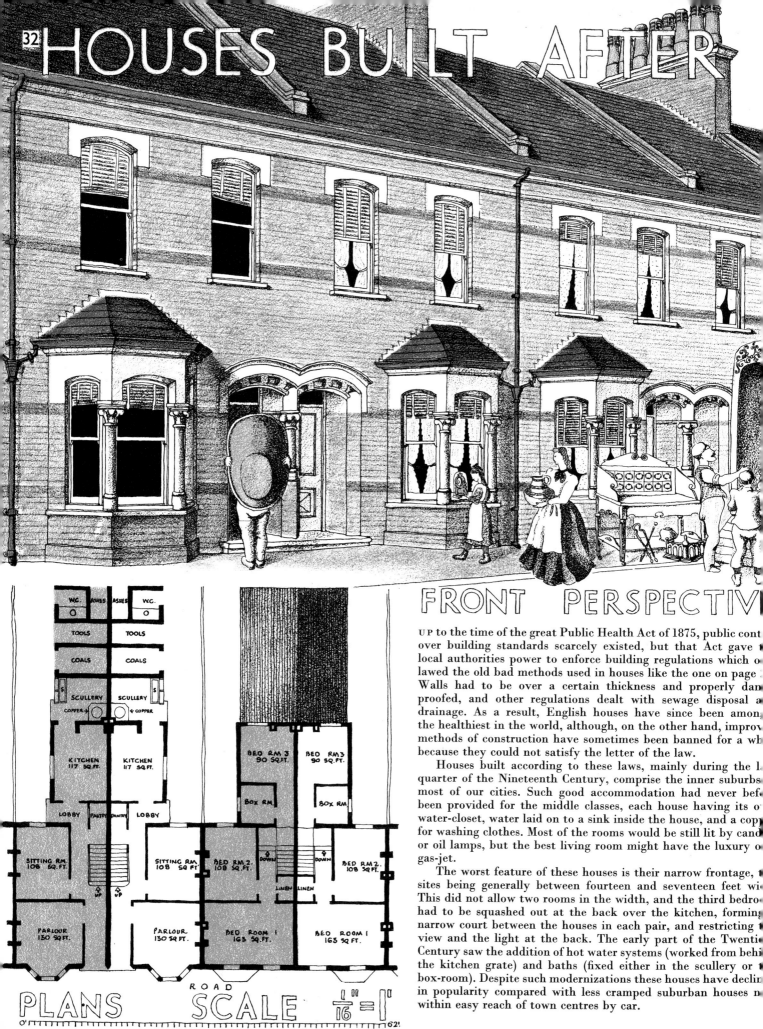

FRONT PERSPECTIVE

Labels on plans:

W.C. ASHES ASHES W.C.
TOOLS — TOOLS
COALS — COALS
SCULLERY — SCULLERY
COPPER → — ← COPPER
KITCHEN 117 SQ.FT. — KITCHEN 117 SQ.FT.
LOBBY — PANTRY PANTRY — LOBBY
SITTING RM. 108 SQ.FT. — SITTING RM. 108 SQ.FT.
UP — UP
PARLOUR 130 SQ.FT. — PARLOUR 130 SQ.FT.

BED RM 3 90 SQ.FT. — BED RM 3 90 SQ.FT.
BOX RM. — BOX RM.
BED RM.2 108 SQ.FT. — DOWN DOWN — BED RM.2 108 SQ.FT.
LINEN LINEN
BED ROOM 1 163 SQ.FT. — BED ROOM 1 163 SQ.FT.

ROAD

PLANS SCALE $\frac{1}{16}'' = 1'$

0' .... 62'

UP to the time of the great Public Health Act of 1875, public cont
over building standards scarcely existed, but that Act gave
local authorities power to enforce building regulations which o
lawed the old bad methods used in houses like the one on page
Walls had to be over a certain thickness and properly dam
proofed, and other regulations dealt with sewage disposal a
drainage. As a result, English houses have since been amon
the healthiest in the world, although, on the other hand, improv
methods of construction have sometimes been banned for a wh
because they could not satisfy the letter of the law.

Houses built according to these laws, mainly during the l
quarter of the Nineteenth Century, comprise the inner suburbs
most of our cities. Such good accommodation had never bef
been provided for the middle classes, each house having its o
water-closet, water laid on to a sink inside the house, and a cop
for washing clothes. Most of the rooms would be still lit by cand
or oil lamps, but the best living room might have the luxury o
gas-jet.

The worst feature of these houses is their narrow frontage,
sites being generally between fourteen and seventeen feet wi
This did not allow two rooms in the width, and the third bedro
had to be squashed out at the back over the kitchen, forming
narrow court between the houses in each pair, and restricting
view and the light at the back. The early part of the Twenti
Century saw the addition of hot water systems (worked from behi
the kitchen grate) and baths (fixed either in the scullery or
box-room). Despite such modernizations these houses have declin
in popularity compared with less cramped suburban houses n
within easy reach of town centres by car.

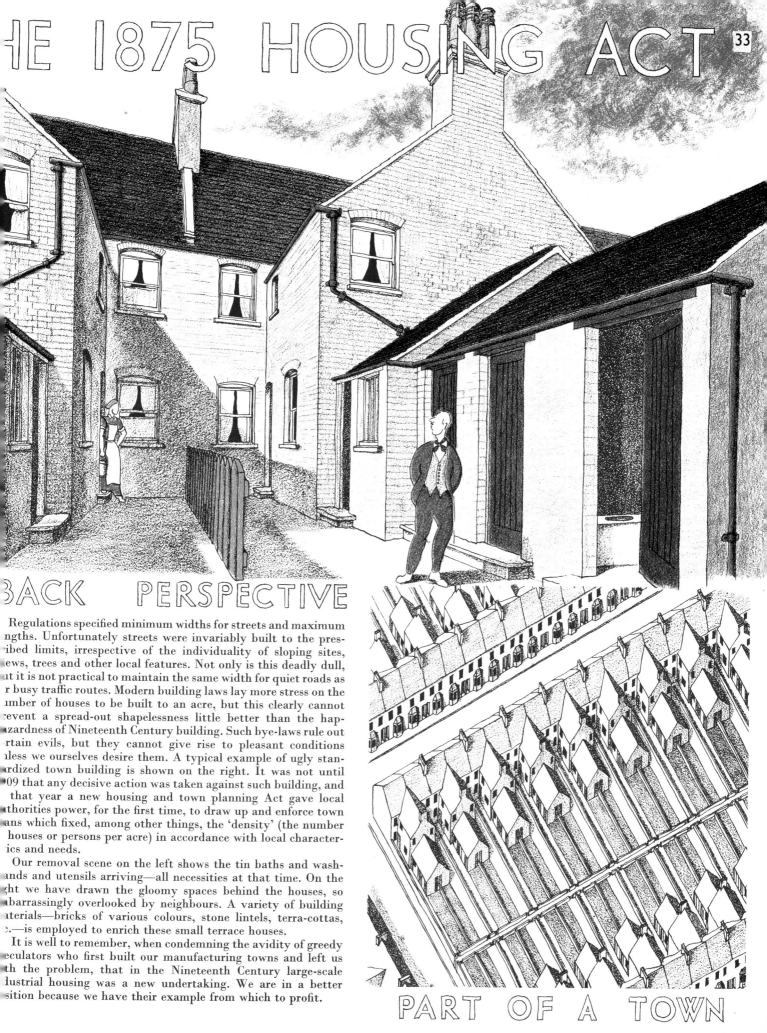

BACK PERSPECTIVE

Regulations specified minimum widths for streets and maximum lengths. Unfortunately streets were invariably built to the prescribed limits, irrespective of the individuality of sloping sites, views, trees and other local features. Not only is this deadly dull, but it is not practical to maintain the same width for quiet roads as for busy traffic routes. Modern building laws lay more stress on the number of houses to be built to an acre, but this clearly cannot prevent a spread-out shapelessness little better than the haphazardness of Nineteenth Century building. Such bye-laws rule out certain evils, but they cannot give rise to pleasant conditions unless we ourselves desire them. A typical example of ugly standardized town building is shown on the right. It was not until 1909 that any decisive action was taken against such building, and in that year a new housing and town planning Act gave local authorities power, for the first time, to draw up and enforce town plans which fixed, among other things, the 'density' (the number of houses or persons per acre) in accordance with local characteristics and needs.

Our removal scene on the left shows the tin baths and washstands and utensils arriving—all necessities at that time. On the right we have drawn the gloomy spaces behind the houses, so embarrassingly overlooked by neighbours. A variety of building materials—bricks of various colours, stone lintels, terra-cottas, etc.—is employed to enrich these small terrace houses.

It is well to remember, when condemning the avidity of greedy speculators who first built our manufacturing towns and left us with the problem, that in the Nineteenth Century large-scale industrial housing was a new undertaking. We are in a better position because we have their example from which to profit.

PART OF A TOWN

THE FIRST OF THE PEABODY BUILDINGS

IT was the activities of Lord Shaftesbury and Edwin Chadwick and other outstanding idealists who fought for better living conditions in the Nineteenth Century which succeeded in persuading Parliament that education, health, housing and, later, town planning, were the responsibility of all. Other reformers were engaged in practical experiments. Octavia Hill organized the rebuilding of slum areas and opened clubs and play-grounds, George Peabody founded a trust for providing better housing conditions, and the East End Dwellings Company began to carry out pioneer flat building in the poorer parts of London. Local authorities were for the first time empowered to build houses themselves by the Housing of the Working Classes Act of 1890, and big schemes were undertaken by the L.C.C. and in Liverpool. Not until the 1920's, however, did municipalities in general go in for building on a large scale.

Flats were used in the Peabody scheme because it was clearly cheaper to build two or three dwellings on a site than one. Our drawing shows the first of the blocks of flats to be built in London in 1868. The secretary of the Trust kindly allowed us to trace the original contract drawings, and from these we drew our plans and set up the birds-eye perspective. The block plan on this page shows the general arrangement. There were three main staircases each giving access to six or seven tenements or flats on the middle three floors. The top floor was used as a communal wash-house, and you will see the row of small windows, which could be opened to make a breeze to dry the clothes hanging in the large drying rooms immediately behind. The coppers were grouped behind the pointed windows, and there are two ventilators in the roof for steam. One arm of the building plan, applicable equally to any floor except the ground and top one, is detailed on the next page. Each flat opens off a communal passage-way, some having two and others one bedroom. Water-closets were provided but they had to be shared, as did the sinks and water supplies. A thoughtful item is the dust-chute, by the stairs on each floor directly over the dust-bins. Compared with slum houses, these flats must have been fine places to live in. Tenants had somewhere to wash clothes, water-closets, indoor water-supply, and a private self-contained suite of rooms. The next step—much later—was to bring the water and sanitary services into each flat, and cut out the communal corridors. How this is now being done is shown on pages 44 and 45.

The Peabody building has solid weight-bearing walls, thick on account of the height, with the roof divided into two spans like the Renaissance houses on pages 24 and 25.

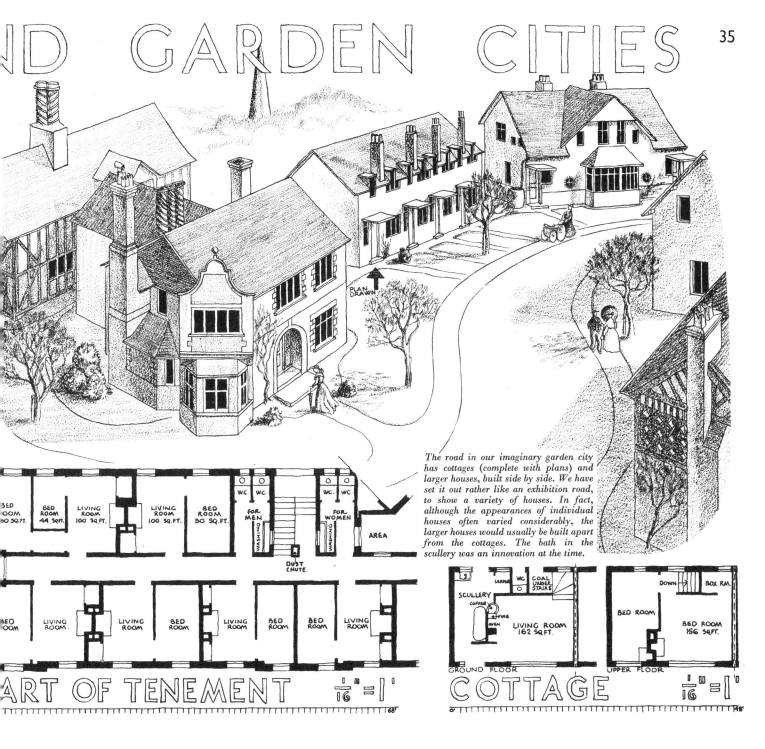

The road in our imaginary garden city has cottages (complete with plans) and larger houses, built side by side. We have set it out rather like an exhibition road, to show a variety of houses. In fact, although the appearances of individual houses often varied considerably, the larger houses would usually be built apart from the cottages. The bath in the scullery was an innovation at the time.

PLAN DRAWN

ART OF TENEMENT $\frac{1}{16}$ = 1'

BED ROOM 50 SQ.FT. · BED ROOM 44 SQ.FT. · LIVING ROOM 100 SQ.FT. · LIVING ROOM 100 SQ.FT. · BED ROOM 50 SQ.FT. · W.C. W.C. FOR MEN · WASHING · DUST CHUTE · WASHING · W.C. W.C. FOR WOMEN · AREA

BED ROOM · LIVING ROOM · LIVING ROOM · BED ROOM · LIVING ROOM · BED ROOM · BED ROOM · LIVING ROOM

COTTAGE $\frac{1}{16}$ = 1'

S · LARDER · WC · COAL UNDER STAIRS · DOWN · BOX RM · SCULLERY · COPPER · FIRE · OVEN · LIVING ROOM 162 SQ.FT. · BED ROOM · BED ROOM 156 SQ.FT. · GROUND FLOOR · UPPER FLOOR

Some reformers, instead of trying to patch up old towns, turned their attention towards building completely new ones. Among earlier odel villages, which led up to the idea of the Garden City, were Edensor in Derbyshire, and the industrial village of Saltaire near Bradford. uch larger projects were Port Sunlight near Liverpool, built by Lord Leverhulme between 1887 and 1910, and Bournville, founded by eorge Cadbury at about the same time. The biggest scheme, the building of the completely new town of Letchworth in Hertfordshire, wes its origin, early in the present century, to the enthusiasm of Ebenezer Howard. The cottage plan we have shown is an early example om Letchworth Garden City. Most of these first garden city schemes were a reaction against the overcrowding of Victorian towns, and nsequently there was more evidence of the garden than of the city. Houses varied in spacing, size and appearance, and so the streets were ten, compared with Georgian work, rather shapeless affairs. Moreover, widely dispersed shops and public buildings spread social life and citement too thinly over a wide area. But the idea caught on rapidly among people sickened by the crowded monotony of bye-law streets d speculative builders soon took it up, finding a ready market for the collections of houses that grew up on the outskirts of all our towns d cities. The garden city planners fixed a size and population limit for their towns such that all inhabitants would be within easy reach of eir work and of the open country; and they provided public buildings and facilities on that scale. Speculative builders fixed no limit, and ten merely succeeded in swallowing up useful country land.

It is claimed for Port Sunlight that there are houses in all styles of English cottage building from the half-timber period onwards, includ- g a replica of the house in which Shakespeare was born. This was all part of a growing romantic interest in pre-industrial England. Old ttage details such as casement windows with leaded panes returned: the fashion inside the house was for antique furniture, and as there re insufficient antiques to go round, there was a flourishing trade in fakes. In the early stages of the movement, modern materials were t needed, and strangely enough when they were later introduced they were used to cheapen the construction of antique style facades: bestos sheets, for example, to get the 'plaster and half timber' effect, and steel beams encased in planks to imitate real wooden beams.

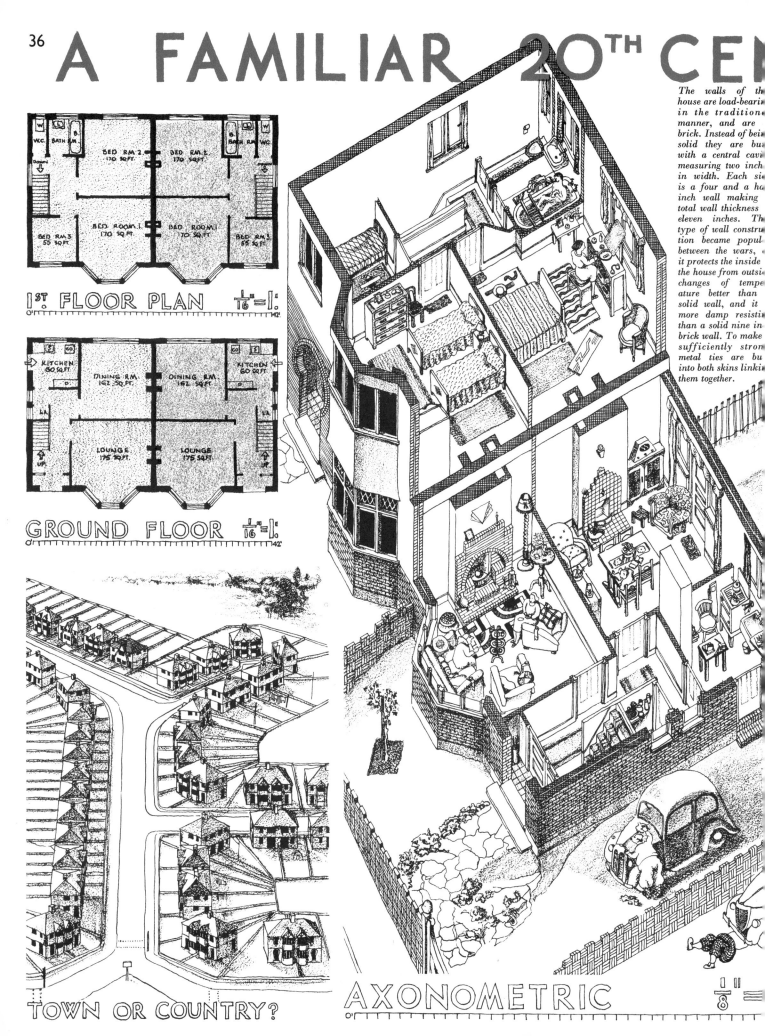

1ˢᵗ FLOOR PLAN $\frac{1"}{16} = 1'$

W.C. BATH RM
BED RM 2.
170 SQ.FT.
BED RM 2.
170 SQ.FT.
BATH RM W.C.

Down
Down

BED RM 3
55 SQ.FT.
BED ROOM I.
170 SQ.FT.
BED ROOM I.
170 SQ.FT.
BED RM 3
55 SQ.FT.

GROUND FLOOR $\frac{1"}{16} = 1'$

KITCHEN
60 SQ.FT.
DINING RM
162 SQ.FT.
DINING RM
162 SQ.FT.
KITCHEN
60 SQ.FT.

LOUNGE
175 SQ.FT.
LOUNGE
175 SQ.FT.

UP
UP

The walls of the house are load-bearing in the traditional manner, and are of brick. Instead of being solid they are built with a central cavity measuring two inches in width. Each side is a four and a half inch wall making a total wall thickness of eleven inches. This type of wall construction became popular between the wars, as it protects the inside of the house from outside changes of temperature better than a solid wall, and it is more damp resisting than a solid nine inch brick wall. To make it sufficiently strong metal ties are built into both skins linking them together.

TOWN OR COUNTRY?

AXONOMETRIC $\frac{1"}{8} =$

PERSPECTIVE VIEW — THE DETAILED HOUSES

THE REMAINING pages deal with examples of Twentieth-century work. Some of the dwellings included are of traditional construction, whilst others give an idea of the possibilities of modern techniques. We have also tried to indicate the solutions that are being offered to some of the housing problems of our day.

As an indication of the general housing position as it existed in 1939, it is worth noting that, according to some pre-war figures nearly half the total number of houses in the whole country were then more than sixty years old; tenements like the Peabody building, bye-law houses, big draughty Victorian mansions (with no servants to keep them clean), 'back-to-backs', and a few houses from Georgian days. In spite of patching-up and improvement many of these houses were completely out of date when compared with what might have taken their place; and some of them were unhealthy and verminous. Nor were there enough of them to go round. A 1933 enquiry into the number of people living in separate houses revealed that a quarter of the population of this country was badly overcrowded. In 1936 a special Act called the Overcrowding Act laid it down that there should not be more than two persons to a room, children under ten counting as half and babies as nil. This is a poor standard when four children may be fitted into a room not counting babies, without breaking the law, but even this low standard could not be enforced because there were not enough houses available. The position after the 1939-1945 war was far worse owing to war damage, disrepair, and to an increase in the number of individual families desiring houses.

There were, in pre-war years, plenty of houses being built of the type illustrated on this page, but the majority were 'For Sale' and many people living in the older houses could not afford to buy, and so the problem remained largely unsolved. Some local authorities built houses to be let at lower rents, but buying land and borrowing money were so expensive that most of the schemes could not afford to provide the shopping centres, libraries and other facilities which everybody wants, and the houses themselves had often to be cut to a very low standard of accommodation. With this fact in mind, the Government made grants to local authorities at specially low rates of interest, and as a result more low rental houses became available. The shortage was so great, however, that some towns still have big house-building programmes to carry out.

Before plans can be drawn up for any house, it is necessary to decide what sized rooms are required. To assist in national planning, the Government appointed a committee to investigate the question of how much space was needed in a house if conditions were to be healthy and comfortable, and room allowed for normal activities and normal fittings and furnishings. In 1944, the Committee recommended the following minimum sizes for rooms:

Living rooms not used for meals	..	160 square feet	Best bedrooms	135 square feet
Living rooms used for meals	..	210 ,, ,,	Second bedrooms	110 ,, ,,
Kitchens used for meals	.. ..	110 ,, ,,	Single bedrooms	70 ,, ,,
Working kitchens only	.. ..	100 ,, ,,		

To compare these with the rooms in your own house, measure the width and length of each room in feet, and multiply the two figures together. Since most of the plans in this book show the area of each room, figured in the middle of the room with the name, you will be able, by comparing these figures with those of your own rooms, to form an impression of the actual size of the rooms illustrated, as well as seeing how they relate to minimum 1944 standards. (It is clear, for instance, that the kitchen in this house is too small, and so is the third bedroom above it). It was also decided that the minimum total area for new houses should be between 900 and 950 square feet, calculated by measuring the area within the external walls on each floor and adding them together. The area for the house on this page is about 1000 square feet.

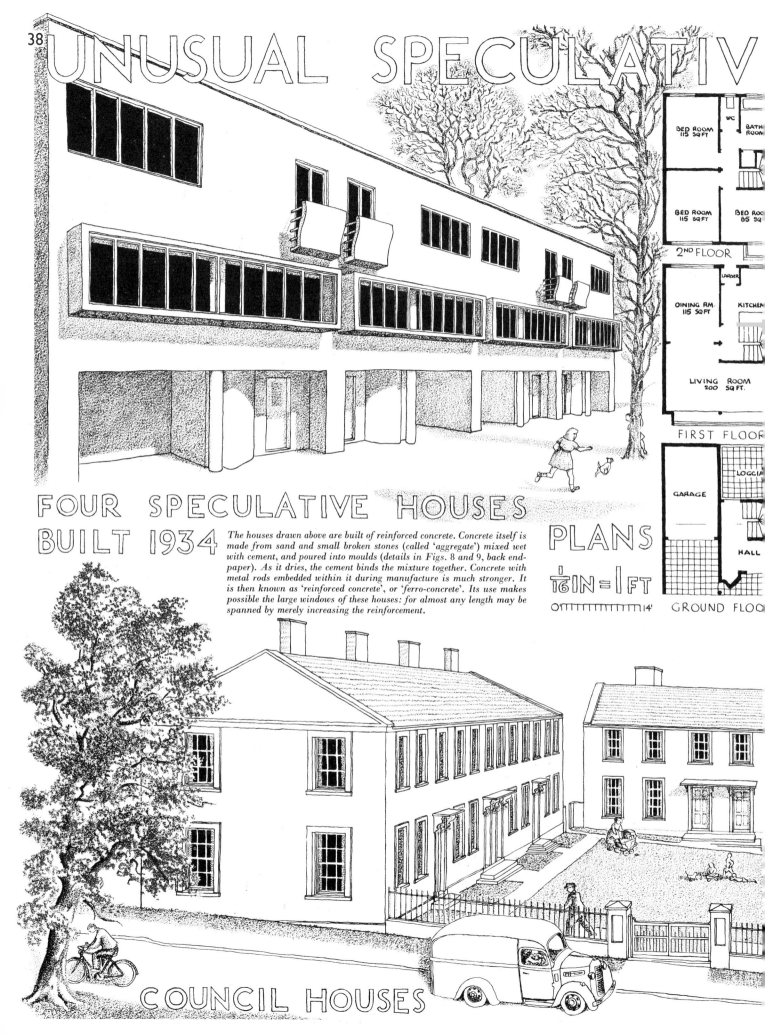

UNUSUAL SPECULATIV

FOUR SPECULATIVE HOUSES BUILT 1934

The houses drawn above are built of reinforced concrete. Concrete itself is made from sand and small broken stones (called 'aggregate') mixed wet with cement, and poured into moulds (details in Figs. 8 and 9, back end-paper). As it dries, the cement binds the mixture together. Concrete with metal rods embedded within it during manufacture is much stronger. It is then known as 'reinforced concrete', or 'ferro-concrete'. Its use makes possible the large windows of these houses: for almost any length may be spanned by merely increasing the reinforcement.

PLANS

1/16 IN = 1 FT

0 ‖‖‖‖‖‖‖‖‖‖‖‖ 14'

BED ROOM 115 SQ FT

WC

BATH ROOM

BED ROOM 115 SQ FT

BED ROOM 85 SQ FT

2ND FLOOR

LARDER

DINING RM. 115 SQ FT

KITCHEN

LIVING ROOM 200 SQ FT.

FIRST FLOOR

GARAGE

LOGGIA

HALL

GROUND FLOOR

COUNCIL HOUSES

COUNCIL HOUSES 1947

PLANNING has not really started when we have decided the sizes of rooms, and the architect is often given this information before he commences work. He then tries to imagine how the proposed building will be used, and arranges the rooms in the most agreeable and convenient way. Architects speak of ordinary routes taken in walking about a building as 'the circulation'. A good house plan has a circulation area consisting of landing, staircase and hall reduced to a minimum. The way rooms face matters very much: how often we hear the complaint that the larder gets all the sun while the living room gets none! The furnishing of a house has also to be considered and, for instance, an architect tries to place windows to suit convenient furniture arrangements indoors, as well as to form an agreeable window pattern outside.

The modern tendency in house design is towards fewer and larger rooms, often capable of sub-division into sections for different purposes. The living room of the Town House on pages 40 and 41 shows this feature, and there is another arrangement of it in the left-hand plan of a prefabricated house on page 42. Advantages claimed for a living room which runs through from front to back (as here) are added interest from looking out in two directions, more light, and possibly more sun and better ventilation. The reinforced concrete houses in the picture to the left have their staircases in the centre of the plan, a great advantage because it leaves both outer walls completely free for the main rooms with large windows. But it is only made possible because the houses have, so to speak, an extra storey *beneath* them, in which is the entrance and access to the stairs; and because they have a flat roof with a sky-light in it above the staircase. The extra storey is also used to contain the garages, saving space at the sides. Alternatively, garages are sometimes built between houses, with neighbouring garages attached and extra rooms above them. Either arrangement avoids the unpleasant 'gap-spacing' illustrated in the familiar type of house on pages 36 and 37.

The layout plan below shows the general arrangement of the council houses which were constructed in 1947 for Yorkshire miners. Most of the houses are grouped round three courtyards, a much tidier layout than the more common haphazard building. It must be pleasant living in these houses with a grass space in front, away from traffic, and a service road for delivering goods at the back. The perspective shows that the buildings themselves are as orderly in design as the layout. The upper windows, spaced equally, make a band. In the same way the eaves, unbroken by bays, suggest unity. This contrasts with the disjointed, unneighbourly, self-assertive building of the familiar Twentieth-century types drawn on pages 36 and 37. The general design of the houses, with their low pitched roofs, covered with large manufactured slabs, the plastered brick walls, coloured buff, is in harmony with local traditional house building. The path to the front doors within the courtyards is made of stone slabs laid in patterns. The plans are of the usual type, where the kitchen is sufficiently large for use at meal-times.

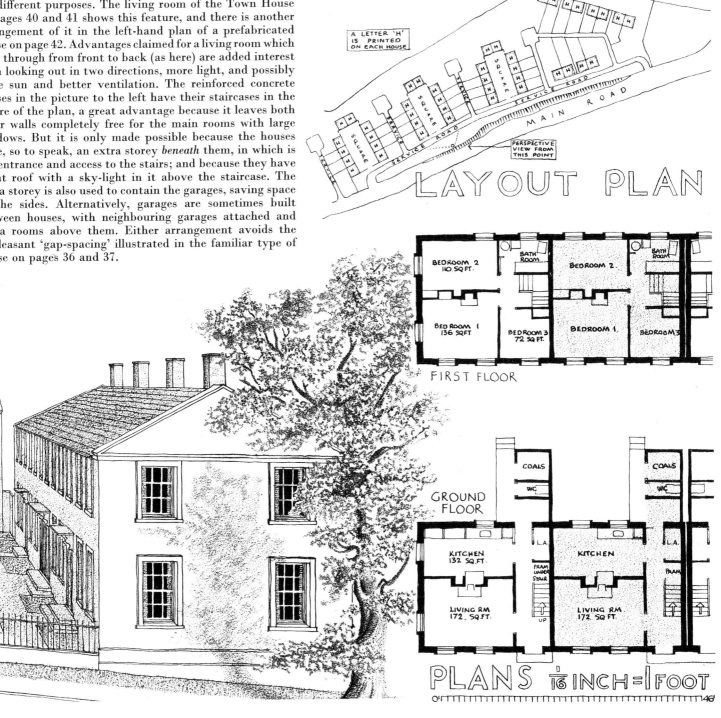

A LETTER 'H' IS PRINTED ON EACH HOUSE

PERSPECTIVE VIEW FROM THIS POINT

LAYOUT PLAN

FIRST FLOOR

BEDROOM 2 110 SQ.FT.
BED ROOM 1 136 SQ.FT.
BEDROOM 3 72 SQ.FT.
BATH ROOM
BEDROOM 2
BEDROOM 1
BEDROOM 3
BATH ROOM

GROUND FLOOR

COALS
WC
KITCHEN 132 SQ.FT.
LIVING RM 172 SQ.FT.
PRAM UNDER STAIR
COALS
WC
KITCHEN
LIVING RM 172 SQ.FT.
PRAM

PLANS 1/16 INCH = 1 FOOT

FIRST FLOOR PLAN
SCALE 1/16" = 1'

GROUND FLOO

This house was specially signed for an artist. A large stu occupies the top floor, a although a comparatively sm house, maids' service and acco modation was required. individualistic house of this s is a luxury, and consequently not properly within the scope this book. It is, however, one of few houses in this country bu with a reinforced concrete fra about which we were able to information in 1947.

PERSPECTIVE VIEW

AS can be seen from the examples we have chosen to illustrate the historical section of the book, choice of shape is to some extent limited by whatever structural method is used; for example, compare the cruck house (pages 12 and 13) and the Yeoman's house (pages 10 and 11). Shape, we have shown, is also limited by individual requirements of the occupants of houses, or in other words the form varies according to function; for example, the house on this page has a special function. Further factors influencing design are fashion and taste, and our pictures throughout give an idea of how builders have followed the fashion in house design. The question arises how we may expect present-day materials, structural systems, requirements and fashions to influence the shape of our new houses.

Many of the old materials can still, of course, be obtained, but even though they may be the best for our purpose, we are often prevented from using them because, being laboriously hand produced (as Cotswold stone is, for instance), they are too costly. Machine-made bricks, artificial stone and an ever-increasing variety of machine-produced synthetic materials take their places. A moment's thought is sufficient to show that, when new materials are used as close neighbours to old ones, the mixture is likely to give pleasure provided the materials do not clash with one another.

Available to us as methods for house construction are (A) the load-bearing wall method and (B) the frame method. The former has already been fully illustrated, and is still the commonest method to-day. The Yorkshire Miners' Cottages on pages 38 and 39 are constructed in this way. Although built with load-bearing walls

the windows are spanned with reinforced concrete lintels. Sin these may be of almost unlimited length, they may give rise to different form of house from the older method in which usual brick arches, in the case of brickwork, and stone lintels, in t case of stone work, both limited the width of the openings benea them. The frame method is on the same principle as the old timb frame construction, but the frame is to-day of steel or reinforce concrete. The left-hand houses on page 38, the house on this pag and the flats on pages 44 and 45 are all of reinforced concrete fra construction. It is not so easy to pick out the frames as it w. in the Sixteenth-century Craftsman's House, because concret mixed in a fluid state, is poured into moulds to set the way we wa it: if we desire a whole wall to act as a post or beam in the frame, can make it that shape. This has actually been the case in t houses on page 38 and in the flats on pages 44 and 45, but they a none the less built on the frame method. Before the war man houses used the load-bearing wall construction and then, sticking planks on the outside wall, faked a timber frame—a devi which shocks us when we know what a real timber-frame buildin looks like. Prefabricated construction makes use of either loa bearing or frame methods, as we shall see on page 43.

We referred to the role of fashion in architecture on page 18 it affected Seventeenth-century buildings. But in fact fashion ha played an important part in house design during the entire perio covered by this book. For instance, choice of window shape an size, and even methods of construction, though governed in pa by builders' skills, were often largely determined by fashion. To-da some of us have our favourite historical building fashions ('styles') rather in the same way that most of us prefer certai clothes or hobbies. Architects are similarly influenced by fashio when they design houses and buildings. Nevertheless, despite th magnetism of fashion we can single out the beautiful in buildin whatever may be the style in which it is expressed. Harmoniou proportions, pleasing textures, the right use of colour—these a some of the factors that make a building beautiful. 'Good taste'– the ability to distinguish what is harmonious, pleasing and 'right and to reject what is not—is a gift worth cultivating. Vernacula builders, the craftsmen who worked in local materials by tradition methods, seem to have acquired such taste instinctively as part their heritage. But to-day tradition has given way to an increasingl chaotic pursuit of novelty for its own sake. Perhaps our schoo could do more to open pupils' eyes to good and bad in architectur as part of the growing realization that our environment is wort caring for.

BED ROOM | BATH | BED ROOM

BED ROOM

NEN | WC | BATH

STUDIO

DOWN

TERRACE

TANKS

ND. FLOOR **3RD. FLOOR**

ROUND, 2ND & 3RD FLOOR PLANS
RAWN TO SCALE OF $\frac{1}{32}$ IN = | FT.

SOMETRIC

CALE $\frac{1}{8}$ IN = 1 FT.

14

n the isometric drawing parts of the walls and roofs of the house have been removed to give an idea of the construction and the appearance within the house. The deep reinforced
ncrete beams which cross the front of the house below the long windows are faced with 6-in. square brown tiles. Only the upper front reinforced concrete walls and the front
rner framework are left exposed and painted white. The sides and rear walls of the house are 11-in. brick cavity wall construction, with the outer skin covering the reinforced
ncrete frame, which shows solid black where it is cut through in section on the isometric drawing. (Roof and floor beams of reinforced concrete are also shown black.) The bay
ndow lighting the dining portion of the living room is constructed of glass bricks in a reinforced concrete frame. In the picture a girl is shown placing crockery in the service
t, which descends within a shaft to the kitchen immediately below, on the ground floor. At each side of the lift shaft, service ducts are visible containing some of the heating,
rvice, and waste pipes. All the pipes are accommodated in this manner instead of appearing on the outside of the building. The hot water heating system and supply is gas
ated, and the radiators in living and bedrooms may be seen below the long windows, placed behind grilles. The owner asked for coal fires in the living room and one bedroom;
d as a flue is provided from the boiler room in the basement below ground level, three flues are shown appearing at roof level on the isometric.

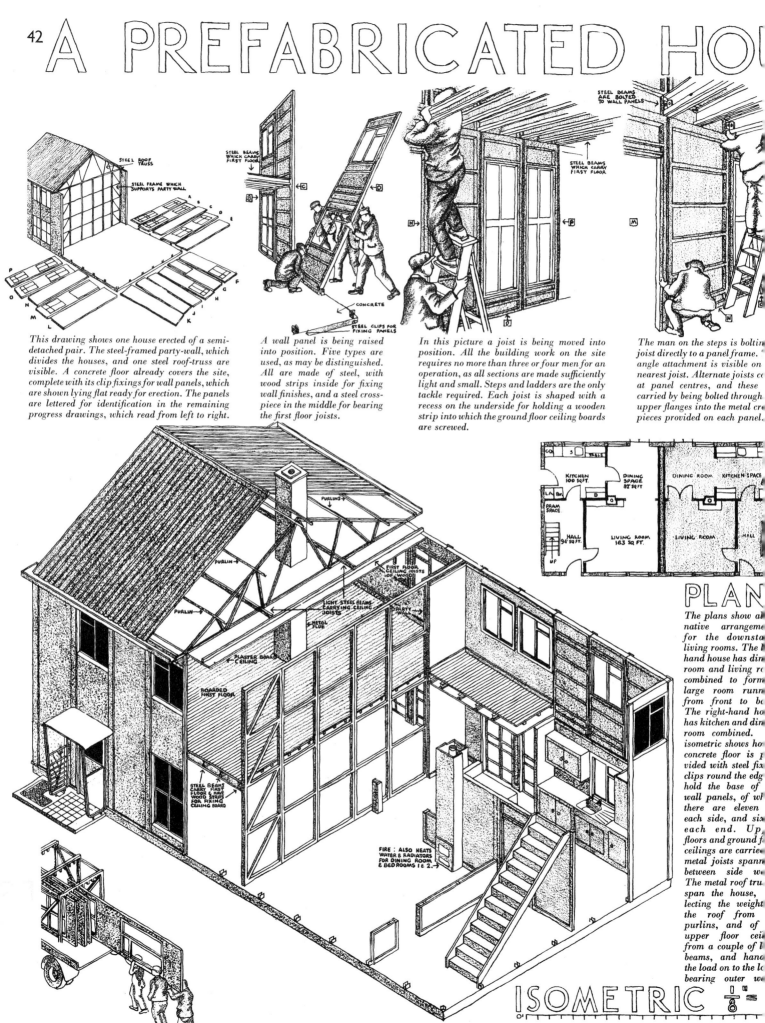

This drawing shows one house erected of a semi-detached pair. The steel-framed party-wall, which divides the houses, and one steel roof-truss are visible. A concrete floor already covers the site, complete with its clip fixings for wall panels, which are shown lying flat ready for erection. The panels are lettered for identification in the remaining progress drawings, which read from left to right.

A wall panel is being raised into position. Five types are used, as may be distinguished. All are made of steel, with wood strips inside for fixing wall finishes, and a steel cross-piece in the middle for bearing the first floor joists.

In this picture a joist is being moved into position. All the building work on the site requires no more than three or four men for an operation, as all sections are made sufficiently light and small. Steps and ladders are the only tackle required. Each joist is shaped with a recess on the underside for holding a wooden strip into which the ground floor ceiling boards are screwed.

The man on the steps is bolti... joist directly to a panel frame. ... angle attachment is visible on ... nearest joist. Alternate joists c... at panel centres, and these ... carried by being bolted through ... upper flanges into the metal cre... pieces provided on each panel.

PLAN

The plans show al... native arrangeme... for the downsta... living rooms. The ... hand house has di... room and living r... combined to form... large room runn... from front to b... The right-hand ho... has kitchen and din... room combined. ... isometric shows ho... concrete floor is p... vided with steel fix... clips round the edg... hold the base of ... wall panels, of wh... there are eleven ... each side, and six ... each end. Up... floors and ground f... ceilings are carrie... metal joists spann... between side w... The metal roof tru... span the house, ... lecting the weight ... the roof from ... purlins, and of ... upper floor cei... from a couple of l... beams, and hand... the load on to the lo... bearing outer we...

ISOMETRIC

is drawing shows all the wall panels in ition, with the exception of four at the . This opening is left until the last, carrying in the roof trusses, two of ich are required to complete the second se of the semi-detached pair. The roof eting is supported directly from the sses by six purlins.

Here is a roof truss in the final stage of erection. One end rests on the wall panelling, while the other is being lifted. The first floor steel joists, already fixed, make a useful platform for the workers. When the remaining rectangular wall panels have been fixed, specially shaped ones are put in above to fill the triangular shape of the gable end, and complete the outside wall.

Here a steel worker is bolting the second truss to the top of a panel. Afterwards the purlins come, and the roof covering may be completed in a short time. The object has been to form a waterproof shell so that the internal finishings—the fixing of plaster-boards, doors, sinks, etc., and the painting—go on whatever the weather.

This represents one of the metal purlin lengths being bolted to a truss. In addition to carrying the roof, the trusses support light steel beams on the underside, which in turn hold up ceiling joists and boards. The whole weight is finally carried by the load-bearing walls.

At the cost of appearing to disregard layout, we have shown two dis-similar houses haphazardly together in a single drawing. The nearer prefabricated house is described on these pages, and the other was designed to enable any number to be joined to make a terrace. The architect said he feared our drawing represented the way some councils might erect them, in an unplanned manner.

PERSPECTIVE

THE term 'Prefabricated' is now applied only to those houses in which the walls and roof are prefabricated in large units before coming on to the site. Prefabrication of parts had been used increasingly between the wars for such items as windows and doors, which were factory-made by special firms and delivered ready for fixing. Prefabricated houses are built in a variety of materials such as wood, steel, concrete and aluminium. The walls of the house on this page are steel, and are made strong enough to be load-bearing. The vertical lines visible on the outside are not a frame, but the metal clips fastening together the structural sections. Other systems do, however, make use of a structural framework, with the wall units designed merely as a skin.

With the more extensive use of glass and reinforced concrete (which are both good conductors of heat) greater attention was paid to the question of heat insulation. Although great progress was made in theory, for many years practice lagged behind. It is, however, now widely recognized that though heat-insulating construction adds to initial building costs, it not only saves money on the future occupant's fuel bills but also adds substantially to the comfort of a house. Some prefabricated houses are heat insulated very effectively, but not all. The houses at the top of page 38 have an inch of cork lining the four inch concrete walls, and it is worth noting that this combination has the same insulation as an eleven inch brick wall.

These prefabricated houses are heated by a single fire which works a small heating system sufficient to warm the whole house. By 1948 some new estates and blocks of flats provided central heating by hot water pipes. In those on pages 44 and 45, there are two radiators to each flat to give 'background' heat, extra heat being obtained from gas or electric fires where it is required.

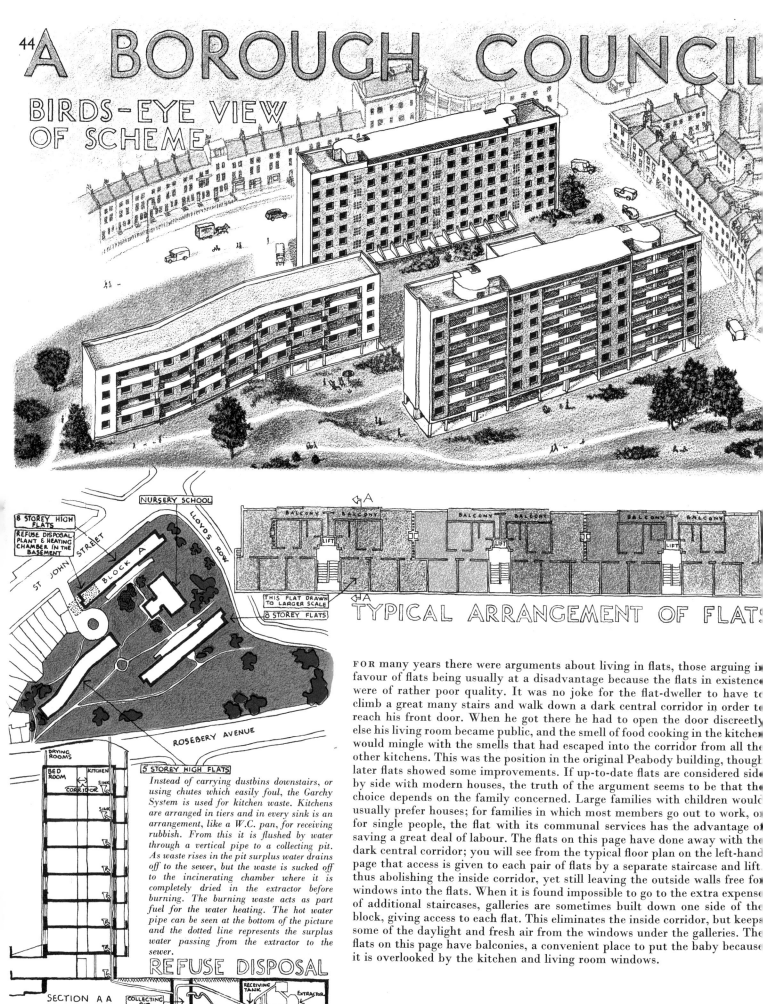

BIRDS-EYE VIEW OF SCHEME

TYPICAL ARRANGEMENT OF FLATS

NURSERY SCHOOL

LLOYDS ROW

8 STOREY HIGH FLATS

REFUSE DISPOSAL PLANT & HEATING CHAMBER IN THE BASEMENT

BLOCK A

ST JOHN STREET

THIS FLAT DRAWN TO LARGER SCALE

8 STOREY FLATS

BALCONY   BALCONY   BALCONY   BALCONY   BALCONY   BALCONY

LIFT   LIFT   LIFT

ROSEBERY AVENUE

5 STOREY HIGH FLATS

DRYING ROOMS

BED ROOM   KITCHEN   SINK

CORRIDOR   SINK

Instead of carrying dustbins downstairs, or using chutes which easily foul, the Garchy System is used for kitchen waste. Kitchens are arranged in tiers and in every sink is an arrangement, like a W.C. pan, for receiving rubbish. From this it is flushed by water through a vertical pipe to a collecting pit. As waste rises in the pit surplus water drains off to the sewer, but the waste is sucked off to the incinerating chamber where it is completely dried in the extractor before burning. The burning waste acts as part fuel for the water heating. The hot water pipe can be seen at the bottom of the picture and the dotted line represents the surplus water passing from the extractor to the sewer.

REFUSE DISPOSAL

SECTION AA   COLLECTING PIT   SEWER   RECEIVING TANK   EXTRACTOR   INCINERATOR

FOR many years there were arguments about living in flats, those arguing in favour of flats being usually at a disadvantage because the flats in existence were of rather poor quality. It was no joke for the flat-dweller to have to climb a great many stairs and walk down a dark central corridor in order to reach his front door. When he got there he had to open the door discreetly else his living room became public, and the smell of food cooking in the kitchen would mingle with the smells that had escaped into the corridor from all the other kitchens. This was the position in the original Peabody building, though later flats showed some improvements. If up-to-date flats are considered side by side with modern houses, the truth of the argument seems to be that the choice depends on the family concerned. Large families with children would usually prefer houses; for families in which most members go out to work, or for single people, the flat with its communal services has the advantage of saving a great deal of labour. The flats on this page have done away with the dark central corridor; you will see from the typical floor plan on the left-hand page that access is given to each pair of flats by a separate staircase and lift, thus abolishing the inside corridor, yet still leaving the outside walls free for windows into the flats. When it is found impossible to go to the extra expense of additional staircases, galleries are sometimes built down one side of the block, giving access to each flat. This eliminates the inside corridor, but keeps some of the daylight and fresh air from the windows under the galleries. The flats on this page have balconies, a convenient place to put the baby because it is overlooked by the kitchen and living room windows.

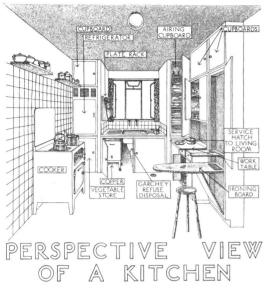

PERSPECTIVE VIEW OF A KITCHEN

Labels in kitchen drawing: CUPBOARD, REFRIGERATOR, AIRING CUPBOARD, CUPBOARDS, PLATE RACK, SERVICE HATCH TO LIVING ROOM, WORK TABLE, IRONING BOARD, COOKER, COPPER, VEGETABLE STORE, GARCHEY REFUSE DISPOSAL

After the war plumbing arrangements generally had made little advance since the Nineteenth Century, which saw such rapid improvements. Much of the plumbing was and still is very unsightly, and periodically, if not continuously, inefficient. Pipes were habitually allowed to disfigure the outsides of buildings, where they may freeze up and burst. In the modern houses illustrated and these flats there is a much better arrangement in which the pipes are grouped together and run in vertical shafts provided for them inside the building. They are out of the way, and they will not freeze. Refuse disposal is another service provided in an improved way in the flats: instead of the chute system installed in the Peabody building, there is the 'Garchy' System, which we have illustrated on page 44.

In 1947 it seemed that, unless an increasing number of people started living in flats, the countryside would disappear completely and the problem of travelling to and from work would become a serious one. If you consider how much space would have been required to build separate houses for all the people who have homes in the blocks of flats we have drawn, you will appreciate how much space can be saved for parks by building more flats in place of houses. Great variety in arrangement is obviously possible if tall blocks of flats are planned in combination with long low terraces, an idea which appealed to some architects of our new towns where it has been developed in attempts to produce pleasing visual effects.

This scheme is part of a much larger scheme in which the architects have taken into account the possible future development of the whole borough. Few comprehensive planning programmes of this kind were carried out for many years. Now, in the 1970's, the improvements they can bring are generally recognized.

Our kitchen drawing shows the view from the doorway. Below the sink draining board, the moveable gas-heated copper can be seen by the side of the Garchy refuse disposal waste pipe. The ironing board is lowered for use, and would otherwise be folded back into the cupboard. The absence of open fires saves space, as no bulky flues and coal storage spaces are required.

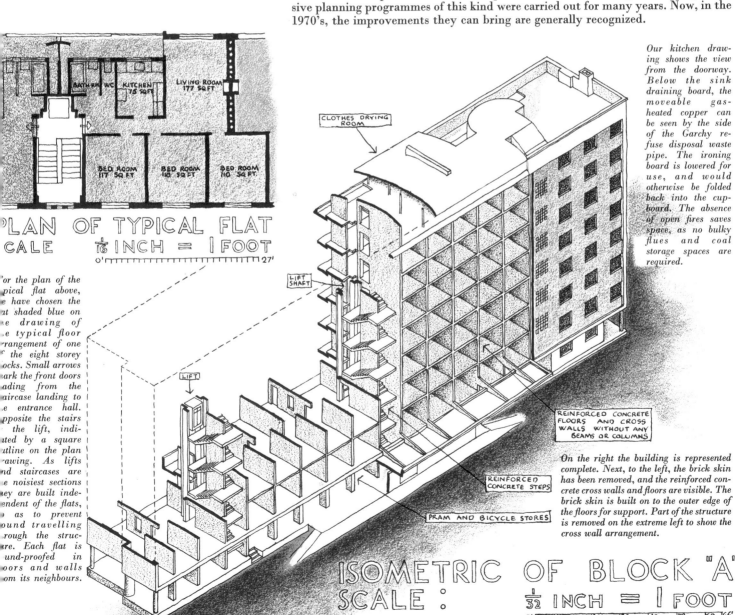

PLAN OF TYPICAL FLAT
SCALE 1/16 INCH = 1 FOOT

0' — 27'

Labels in plan: BATH RM WC, KITCHEN 75 SQ FT, LIVING ROOM 177 SQ FT, BED ROOM 117 SQ FT, BED ROOM 110 SQ FT, BED ROOM 110 SQ FT

For the plan of the typical flat above, we have chosen the flat shaded blue on the drawing of the typical floor arrangement of one of the eight storey blocks. Small arrows mark the front doors leading from the staircase landing to the entrance hall. Opposite the stairs is the lift, indicated by a square outline on the plan drawing. As lifts and staircases are the noisiest sections they are built independent of the flats, so as to prevent sound travelling through the structure. Each flat is sound-proofed in floors and walls from its neighbours.

Labels in isometric drawing: CLOTHES DRYING ROOM, LIFT SHAFT, LIFT, REINFORCED CONCRETE FLOORS AND CROSS WALLS WITHOUT ANY BEAMS OR COLUMNS, REINFORCED CONCRETE STEPS, PRAM AND BICYCLE STORES

On the right the building is represented complete. Next, to the left, the brick skin has been removed, and the reinforced concrete cross walls and floors are visible. The brick skin is built on to the outer edge of the floors for support. Part of the structure is removed on the extreme left to show the cross wall arrangement.

ISOMETRIC OF BLOCK "A"
SCALE : 1/32 INCH = 1 FOOT

0' — 10 — 20 — 30 — 40 — 50 — 60 — 66'

The Brandon Estate. The new square of four-storey dwellings: two lower floors to one row of maisonettes and two upper floors for another row. All principal rooms are planned to have sun, yet all entrances are from the square.

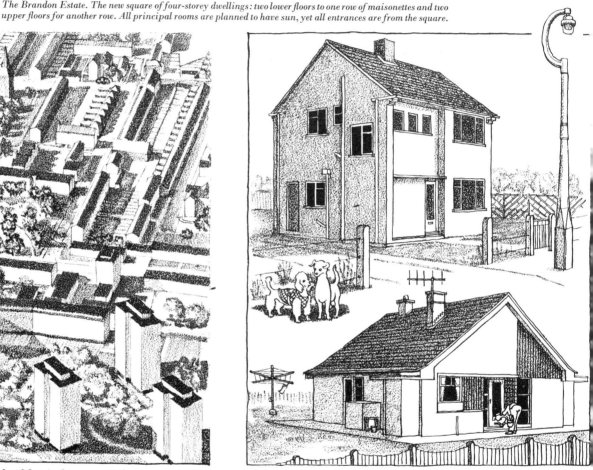

The Brandon Estate: tower blocks of flats in front, square of maisonettes in mid-distance with houses and old church steeple in background.

The house (above): placing of windows of various sizes, and pipes, make for confused appearance; and in the bungalow (below) materials give a 'bitty' appearance.

NOW if we turn to the layout planning of dwellings built since 1948, we find that, despite efforts made to control development, much has been on a par with the piecemeal estate planning of pre-war days. Notable exceptions there were, thank goodness. Among them London County Council housing schemes now enjoy a world-wide reputation for excellence. One of the most famous is perhaps that at Roehampton. The Brandon Estate, built in South London in 1960, incorporates modernized Nineteenth-century houses, tower blocks of flats, maisonettes, houses, old people's homes, public buildings, an old church steeple which has become a land-mark, and a square. This was the first square to be built in London for very many years, something which makes us wonder why in recent times we seem to have avoided regular geometrical shapes like circuses, squares and crescents when the historical ones we have give so much pleasure.

Central area rebuilding accounts for only part of the new work: much also has gone on on the outskirts of our towns, though attempts at the creation of so-called 'green belts' led to the introduction of something known as 'overspill' development— instead of new houses being added at the edges of big cities they are built onto neighbouring villages and small towns, or form part of new towns. But in any case more countryside disappears, urban sprawl increases and transport problems tend to become more acute. In the 1950's an attempt was made to find an alternative scheme for replanning and rebuilding one of London's dormitory suburbs, Boston Manor. As it proved possible to double the existing population, and provide shopping and social facilities then lacking, it appears to have been a good idea. The same treatment could be applied to more centrally situated areas of towns.

Of recent years, more thought has been given to the need to provide more varied accommodation to suit families of different sizes, bachelors, and old people. By 1960 it would have been true to say that never had so many enjoyed so high a standard of material comfort. Yet houses then were often still inadequately heated, their windows and doors gave insufficient protection against the climate and the plumbing still festooned the outer walls. Since 1948 most villages have had additions which unfortunately often give the impression of having been carried out with complete disregard for rural setting and vernacular building tradition.

In external appearance the best of the new houses need fear no comparison; but many are markedly inferior to numbers of

Kitchen and bathrooms are planned centrally as a plumbing unit (leaving external walls free for living and bedrooms) lit and ventilated from clear storey. Pipe duct passes through base of bedroom and bathroom cupboards. These cupboards also assist towards sound-proofing adjoining rooms. Other features of the plan include a conservatory-cum-dining room (visible from kitchen), sound-proof library, and a garage connected to the house, with top-hung doors at both ends and covered car-port beyond.

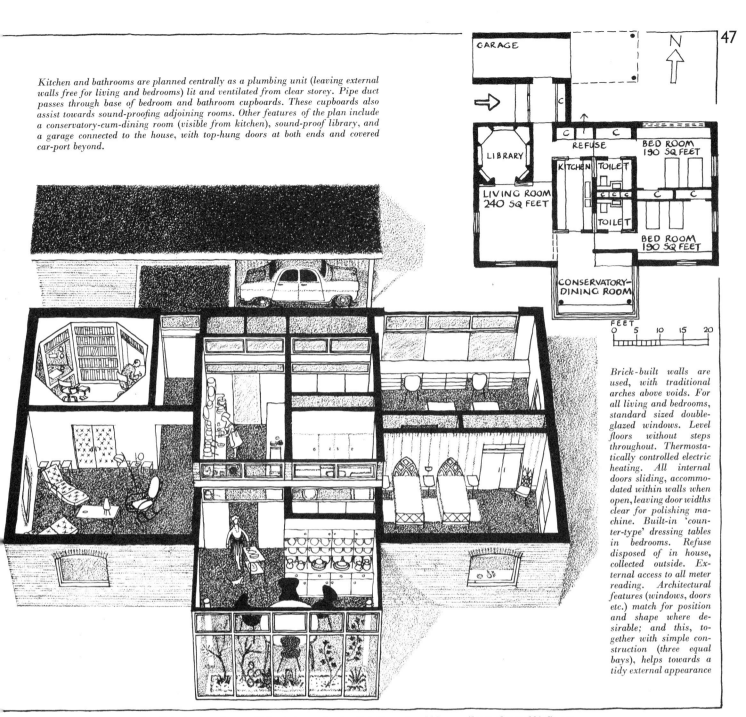

Brick-built walls are used, with traditional arches above voids. For all living and bedrooms, standard sized double-glazed windows. Level floors without steps throughout. Thermostatically controlled electric heating. All internal doors sliding, accommodated within walls when open, leaving door widths clear for polishing machine. Built-in 'counter-type' dressing tables in bedrooms. Refuse disposed of in house, collected outside. External access to all meter reading. Architectural features (windows, doors etc.) match for position and shape where desirable; and this, together with simple construction (three equal bays), helps towards a tidy external appearance

Small single-storey house with two bedrooms (each with bathroom) and library. Above: plan and bird's-eye perspective from south with house roof removed, and below: bird's-eye perspective from same side.

urviving vernacular and other old houses. Look, for instance, at he two dwellings on page 46. The placing of the windows of the ouse looks far from neat. The bungalow has an odd timber oarded affair as part of its front gable, and elsewhere tiles, bricks nd more boards tend towards a confusing effect.

The 1950's saw but few structural changes in house building. ˀrefabrication, which seemed to promise so much just after the var, suffered a temporary check. At that time the organization o provide continuous and large-scale housing orders did not xist. Otherwise prefabrication should have been as successful in ouse construction as in school building. Only during the last lecade were local authorities, working in groups, able to develop nore logical house-building methods, making extensive use of nass-produced building elements.

By the mid 1960's it was clear that there were two approaches: ither through the use of proprietary methods, or by the appli-ation of component building. Components possessed the advan-age of being produced by different firms and of different materials.

But it had also become clear that if the new building methods vere to succeed the number of measurements of the building lements must be reduced and standardized.

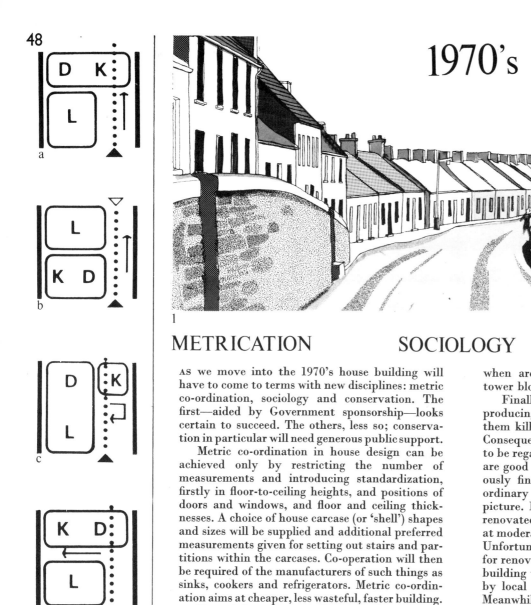

1

1970's

METRICATION   SOCIOLOGY   CONSERVATION

AS we move into the 1970's house building will have to come to terms with new disciplines: metric co-ordination, sociology and conservation. The first—aided by Government sponsorship—looks certain to succeed. The others, less so; conservation in particular will need generous public support.

Metric co-ordination in house design can be achieved only by restricting the number of measurements and introducing standardization, firstly in floor-to-ceiling heights, and positions of doors and windows, and floor and ceiling thicknesses. A choice of house carcase (or 'shell') shapes and sizes will be supplied and additional preferred measurements given for setting out stairs and partitions within the carcases. Co-operation will then be required of the manufacturers of such things as sinks, cookers and refrigerators. Metric co-ordination aims at cheaper, less wasteful, faster building.

By sociology we mean the study, for example, of those housing conditions likely to produce loneliness, insufficient privacy and too few chances to potter and play—drawbacks too little foreseen when architects and planners fell in love with tower blocks and open-plan layouts.

Finally, conservation. The increased costs of producing traditional materials and building with them killed craft building long before the 1970's. Consequently, old cottages and houses have come to be regarded as irreplaceable antiques. But there are good reasons for preserving not only the obviously fine old buildings but many of the more ordinary old houses which help to create the street picture. Furthermore, old buildings can often be renovated to provide good quality accommodation at moderate cost compared with new construction. Unfortunately, at present, Government subsidies for renovating the old lag behind those granted for building the new. More specialized staff is needed by local authorities contemplating conservation. Meanwhile old and irreplaceable buildings disappear continuously. The main hope for preserving the best of the past now lies in the hands of our civic and amenity societies, who need all the help we can give.

Fig. 1. Shore Road cottages, Portaferry, Northern Ireland —craft-built structures of rubble and slate. Though at present providing sub-standard accommodation they could be modernized. Efforts are being made to save them, so far unsuccessfully.

Fig. 2. (f) shows a 6.600 × 6.600 m house shell and (a) to (e) indicate the various possibilities within this shell. L=living room, D=dining room, K=kitchen.

Fig. 3. A few of a large range of differently shaped shells; the figures in the shells show persons housed in each. Blacked shells are those which suit various basic structural needs.

Fig. 4. 300 mm grid lines on part of a drawing of a house. Standard measurements cover wall thickness (SS), roof (RR) and floor (FF) depths, and window height (WW).

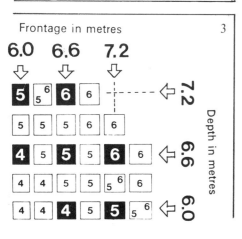

2

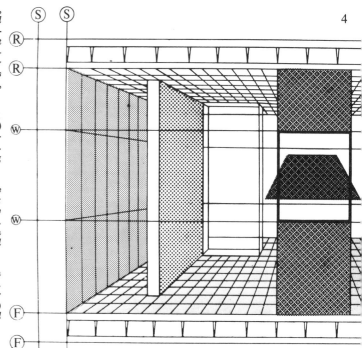

4

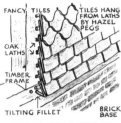

① WATTLE & DAUB

Labels: MUD COATED WITH LIME PLASTER; HAZEL RODS; TIMBER FRAME; HOLES OR SLOTS FOR VERTICALS

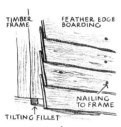

② TILE HANGING

Labels: FANCY TILES; TILES HANG FROM LATHS BY HAZEL PEGS; OAK LATHS; TIMBER FRAME; TILTING FILLET; BRICK BASE

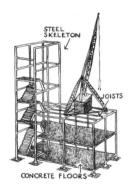

③ WEATHERBOARDING

Labels: TIMBER FRAME; FEATHER EDGE BOARDING; NAILING TO FRAME; TILTING FILLET

④

Labels: STEEL SKELETON; JOISTS; CONCRETE FLOORS

⑤ STEEL FRAME

Labels: STEEL SCAFFOLDING; EXTERNAL SKIN WALL

Fig. 1. WATTLE AND DAUB

A form of construction known as 'Wattle and Daub' was most frequently used for filling in the panels of timber-framed buildings. The basis was formed by springing wattles into holes or slots provided in the horizontal members of the wooden frame. Infilling commenced by weaving twigs or light wattles in and out of the uprights, to form a kind of hurdling. To this was applied on both sides a mixture of clay and chopped straw which obtained key or hold in the hurdling. Lime plaster was sometimes used for a final coat. Part of the outer surface is removed here to show construction. The stone base was necessary to preserve the wooden structure. Sometimes walls were built with a double row of uprights, as in the Peasant's House on pages 12 and 13, and the mud and chopped straw was packed between the uprights.

Fig. 2. TILE HANGING

Tile hanging seems to have been first used for water-proofing old timber-framed buildings, when the wattle and daub panels had become leaky. Oak laths were then often nailed across frame and panel alike, and tiles hung from them, with wooden pins, and usually bedded in lime mortar (a mixture of quick lime, sand and water) with hair added for binding. It was commonest in Sussex, Surrey, Kent and Berkshire during the late Seventeenth Century, when supplies of tiles became more abundant. Frequently, the lower storey was cased with brickwork up to the jetty, and the first floor tile hung. Tiles were made and hung in a variety of patterns, one of which is shown in our drawing. Below the lowest course of tiles a tilting fillet was required for keeping the bottom row tight against those above.

Fig. 3. WEATHERBOARDING

Weatherboarding is a method of covering a timber-framed building with horizontal boards, usually deal, oak, or elm. Boards vary in size and shape, commonest being those cut to a feather edge and laid with the thinner (or feather) edge uppermost, and lapped by the next course of boarding, as shown in our drawing. The boards are fixed by nailing through to the frame immediately above the lap. A usual board size is 7-in. deep, $\frac{3}{4}$ of an inch thick, tapered to $\frac{1}{4}$ of an inch, with a lap of about 3-in. Amongst the earliest buildings constructed with boards are the windmills and watermills of the Eastern Counties. Most of the weather-boarded houses that remain were built during the Eighteenth or early Nineteenth Centuries, and often have classical enrichments, as, for example, House F on page 9.

Figs. 4 & 5. STEEL FRAME

Load-bearing walls were used after the abandonment of the timber frame. But in recent years the frame method has returned. This time a steel or concrete skeleton is used. There are no steel-framed buildings in this book, but several have concrete frames. Concrete beams and columns may be varied in shape to suit particular designs (so that a column may take the shape of a complete wall, or a beam a whole floor), and consequently are less recognisable as frame buildings. We have, therefore, preferred to illustrate stages in the erection of a building with a frame of steel. Frames have not been greatly used in house construction: except where large or continuous windows have been required (as in the houses on pages 38, 40 and 41), or when the designer wants the upper floor plan dissimilar from the ground floor. For in a framed building all light partitions are supported on the floor

⑥ BRICKLAYING

Labels: METAL TIE; LINE; 11" CAVITY WALL; BRICKS BOXED READY FOR USE; MORTAR; SPOT BOARD

⑦ BRICKLAYING TOOLS

Labels: CLUB HAMMER; BRICK COURSE MARKINGS; LINE & PINS; BRICK TROWEL; BOASTER; SPIRIT LEVEL; BRICK HAMMER; PLUMB RULE; STOREY OR GAUGE ROD

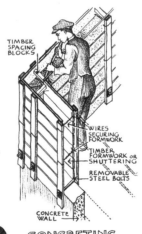

⑧ CONCRETING

Labels: TIMBER SPACING BLOCKS; WIRES SECURING FORMWORK; TIMBER FORMWORK OR SHUTTERING; REMOVABLE STEEL BOLTS; CONCRETE WALL

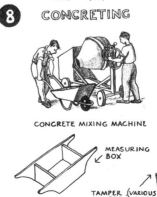

⑨ CONCRETING TOOLS

Labels: CONCRETE MIXING MACHINE; MEASURING BOX; TAMPER (VARIOUS SHAPES MADE)

itself, and heavier ones carried on beams; either case they are independent of the fl[oor] below. To-day frame construction is alwa[ys] used for larger buildings, including flats, [be]cause space is saved by the absence of bu[lky] load-bearing walls on lower floors. It is a[lso] quicker and cheaper. Fig. 4 shows a st[eel] frame building in process of erection, w[ith] the concrete floors for ground and first fl[oor] already in position. In Fig. 5 the framewo[rk] and floors are completed, with the outer s[kin] wall and partitions raised to above third fl[oor] window level. The outer wall is supported [at] each floor level by the beams in the framewo[rk] —it carries no weight, and is merely a shi[eld] to exclude cold and wet weather.

Figs. 6 & 7 BRICKLAYING

Bricks are made from ground clay with wa[ter] added, moulded to a shape 9-in. long, $4\frac{1}{2}$-[in.] wide, and 3-in. deep, and burnt in kil[ns.] Mortar for jointing is often quick lime, sa[nd] and water mixed (called lime mortar). [A] labourer 'boxes' bricks, arranges lime mor[tar] on a 'spot board'. Bricklayers commence t[he] building by raising the corners, testing th[em] to see if the work is vertical with a 'plu[mb] rule', and using the 'spirit level' for ho[ri]zontal checking. They use a 'gauge rod', w[ith] joint thicknesses marked, to get all joints a[nd] courses correctly spaced. Next are built [up] courses of brickwork between corners, 'l[ine] and pins' being used to enable each brick t[o] set truly. One pin is inserted in a verti[cal] joint near the top. The line is stretched ti[ght] from corner to corner, and the second p[in] inserted in the corresponding joint. The l[ine] is made level with the top of the course n[ext] to be built. A 'brick trowel' is used for ha[nd]ling mortar, a 'club hammer' and 'boaster' [for] cutting bricks; and for trueing shapes a[nd] tapping bricks to position, a 'brick hamm[er'].

Figs. 8 & 9. CONCRETING

Concrete is an artificial stone made by bin[d]ing together a mass of broken stone and sa[nd] (both called 'aggregate') with cement a[nd] water. Good aggregate is of shape and s[ize] that packs tightly, leaving few voids. Co[m]mon proportions for concrete are: [one] volume of cement, two of sand, three to f[our] of broken stone. For measuring aggregat[e a] bottomless box (Fig. 9) with handles is us[ed,] easily lifted clear after use. On small j[obs] mixing is by shovel, and on a larger scale [by] mechanical mixer, with a rotating dru[m,] power or hand-driven (Fig. 9). A[fter] thorough mixing the wet concrete is pou[red] into moulds, called formwork, or shutter[ing,] to set. Formwork may be constructed [in] several ways; we show (Fig. 8) a sim[ple] method, using planks tied together w[ith] bolts, wires and vertical studs, and spa[ced] with blocks. To dismantle, the bolts a[re] knocked out, the wire cut back, and the w[all] surface cemented up. Concrete must [be] rammed or 'tamped' before setting if it i[s to] be dense and strong. The workman in Fig[. 8] is 'tamping' concrete.

Fig. 10. OPENINGS IN WALLS

For spanning openings in brick walls arc[hes] are commonly used, either of specia[lly] moulded bricks which together form a wed[ge]-like shape (A), or of common bricks ([B]). Stone walls have large flat stones ca[lled] lintels over openings (C) and (D) or ar[ches] may be used, either semi-circular shaped [(E)] or pointed (F). Concrete walls may be b[uilt] in one piece, or fabricated in sections. [If] reinforcement is used (dotted line in G), [it is] buried within the concrete. The principle [of] reinforced concrete is: concrete resists co[m]pression but is weak in resisting tensi[on]